English Unlimited

A2 Elementary
Self-study Pack (Workbook with DVD-ROM)

Maggie Baigent, Chris Cavey & Nick Robinson

CAMBRIDGE
UNIVERSITY PRESS

CAMBRIDGE UNIVERSITY PRESS
Cambridge, New York, Melbourne, Madrid, Cape Town,
Singapore, São Paulo, Delhi, Mexico City

Cambridge University Press
The Edinburgh Building, Cambridge CB2 8RU, UK

www.cambridge.org
Information on this title: www.cambridge.org/9780521697743

First published 2010
4th printing 2012

Printed in the United Kingdom at the University Press, Cambridge

A catalogue record for this publication is available from the British Library

ISBN 978-0-521-69774-3 Elementary Self-study Pack (Workbook with DVD-ROM)
ISBN 978-0-521-69772-9 Elementary Coursebook with e-Portfolio
ISBN 978-0-521-69776-7 Elementary Teacher's Pack (Teacher's Book with DVD-ROM)
ISBN 978-0-521-69775-0 Elementary Class Audio CDs

Contents

1 People in your life

VOCABULARY

VOCABULARY

People you know

1 Write the words in order to complete the conversation.

JOSEPH	Hello, Catia!
CATIA	Hi, Joseph! Hello, Peter. ¹is / Karima, / colleague / work / This / my / from / . *This is Karima, my colleague from work.*
JOSEPH	²to / Nice / meet / you / .
PETER	Hello. Sorry, ³what's / again / name / your / ?
KARIMA	Karima.
PETER	Hello, Karima.
CATIA	⁴an / Joseph / old / is / friend _____ , Karima. We were at university together.
KARIMA	⁵you / Peter / Are / colleagues / and _____ , Joseph?
JOSEPH	No. We're students on an Arabic course.

Over to you

How do *you* greet people when you meet them for the first time? Write a sentence.

GRAMMAR

be present: *am*, *is*, *are*

2 Complete what Roland says using the words in the box.

are   isn't   'm   'm   'm   'm not   's   's   's   's   's   's

Roland, France

¹I *'m* ___ Roland. ²I ___ from France. My parents ³ ___ called Olivier and Virginie. ⁴Olivier ___ my father and ⁵Virginie ___ my mother. ⁶I ___ single, ⁷I ___ married. My wife's ⁸name ___ Zoé. Serge is my brother. Serge ⁹ ___ married, but he has got a girlfriend. Her ¹⁰name ___ Nathalie. My sister's name is Odette. ¹¹She ___ married to Sébastien. Sébastien and Odette have a son – his ¹²name ___ André.

3 Write the people from Exercise 2 in the family tree.

1 *Olivier* 2 _____

3 *Roland* 4 _____ 4 _____ 6 _____ 7 _____

8 _____

4 Complete what Michio and Csilla say using the expressions in the boxes.

badly paid boring different every day great

I love my job!

difficult easy interesting same every day terrible

I hate my job!

Michio is a primary school teacher.

I work in a lovely school. It's hard work and
¹ *badly paid*, but I love my job. It's never
² _____ because it's ³ _____ .
I think my job is ⁴ _____ !

Csilla is an office manager.

I'm a manager in a big office, and my job
is ⁵ _____ . The work's not
⁶ _____ . In fact, it's ⁷ _____ ,
but it's the ⁸ _____ , and it's not very
⁹ _____ . I really want a new job!

GRAMMAR

be past and present

Monifa, Egypt

5 Monifa talks about her friend Halima. (Circle) the correct words.

This is about my friend Halima. She ¹'s / 're Egyptian – like me – and she ²'s / 're about 30 years old. We ³'s / 're very good friends. We both work as teachers, but we ⁴'re / 're not colleagues. I work in a school in Luxor, and Halima lives in Cairo. We ⁵was / were at school together. Later, we ⁶was / were at the same university, but we ⁷were / weren't in the same class. I ⁸was / were an art student, and she ⁹was / were in the maths department. Now I ¹⁰'m / 's an art teacher, and she ¹¹'m / 's a maths teacher. We ¹²'s / 're still good friends after 20 years.

Over to you

Write a similar paragraph about someone you know well.

MYEnglish

6 Read the text. Are the sentences true or false?

" My name's Halima and I'm a teacher in Cairo, the capital city of Egypt. I'm a teacher in an international school. I teach maths, but my classes are in English. In Egypt, we speak Arabic. It's very different from English. We don't have the verb *be* in the present tense, and we don't have *a* or *an* either. Writing is difficult for young students, because our Arabic writing is different. But my students watch TV in English and they speak good English. I speak English with some of my American colleagues at work. I have some English friends in Cairo, too. I love to show them around my city and to speak English with them. "

Halima, Egypt

1 Halima is an English teacher.   TRUE / FALSE
2 Halima's students watch TV in English.   TRUE / FALSE
3 Halima speaks English to some of her friends.   TRUE / FALSE

7 **Here are some sentences written by Egyptian students. Put the correct form of *be* (*am, is* or *are*) in the correct place in the sentences.**

is
1 My brother /\ a student.

2 My parents teachers.

3 The boy very tall.

4 I a journalist.

5 Jane and I sisters.

Your English

8 Halima says that Arabic doesn't have the verb *be* in the present tense. What differences do you know between your language and English?

EXPLORE Writing

www.mailpals.net

Make new email friends around the world!

Post your message now!

9 Read Susi's message on Mailpals. Circle the correct words.

1 She wants to write to English-speaking / German-speaking friends.
2 Susi speaks good / a little English.

File Edit View Favorites Tools Help

Address www.mailpals.net

www.m@ilpals.net

Posted on: April 01, 05:27:53 PM

Name: Susanne
Email: susi_1980@gmx.net
Age: 28
From: Austria
Seeking: English-speaking friends
Hobbies: Reading, swimming, animals, nature
Comments / Remarks: Hi! I'm Susi, and I'd like to write to people from all over the world. I'm from Salzburg, a small town in Austria, so I speak German, of course! My English is not very good, but I want to learn it. Thank you for your emails.

---

10 Read Blerta's reply. Tick the information that Blerta includes.

1	her age	✓	5	her job	☐
2	where she's from	☐	6	her friends	☐
3	married?	☐	7	her husband's job	☐
4	her hobbies	☐	8	where she lives	☐

Hi, Susi

My name's Blerta. I'm from Tirana, the capital of Albania, but now I live in Berat. This is me in the photo with my husband Arben. We're both 27 years old. We were students at school together! Now Arben is a cook in his family's restaurant, and I'm a shop assistant. My job's quite hard, and it's not well paid, but it's OK.

I don't speak English very well, but can we be email friends?

Please write to me!

Bye!

Blerta

11 Complete these sentences.

1 My _____name's_____ Blerta.
2 I'm _____ Tirana.
3 I live _____ Berat.
4 We're both 27 _____ .
5 ... but _____ we be email friends?
6 Please write _____ me!

12 Write an email message to Susi. Include some of the information from Exercise 10.

1   Before you watch, complete this sentence about yourself.

> I'm from _____,
> and I speak _____.

2   Watch the video. Is anyone from your country?
    Does anyone speak the same languages as you?

3   Watch again and complete the information using the words in the box.

Italy   London, England   India   ~~Bogotá, Colombia~~   Poland   Istanbul in Turkey

1 Luis

I come from _Bogotá, Colombia_____.

2 Justyna

I'm from _____.

3 Monica

I'm originally from _____.

4 Hitin

I'm from _____.

5 Nilgun

I come from _____.

6 Amanda

I'm Amanda Taylor from
_____.

4   Write the correct languages.

1   Poland   _Polish___

2   Turkey   _____

3   Italy   _____

4   France   _____

5   Germany   _____

6   Spain   _____

7   Greece   _____

8   Russia   _____

5   Read the sentences in columns A and B. Which sentences mean 'I speak this
    language very well' and which mean 'I speak this language a bit, not very well'?

A
I speak Spanish.
I'm *fluent* in English.
My *native language* is Hindi.

B
I speak *a bit of* Italian.
I speak *basic* French.
I speak *a little bit of* Russian.

6   Read what Martina says. Then write about you. What is your name?
    Where are you from? What languages do you speak?

> My name is Martina Mettgenberg, and I am from Germany.
> I speak English and German and basic French and basic Hindi.

GLOSSARY

basic (adjective): very simple
a bit (noun): a small amount
fluent (adjective): able to use a language naturally without stopping or making mistakes
native (adjective): Your **native language** is the first language you learn.
originally (adverb): at the beginning or before any changes

2 Away from home

VOCABULARY
Offers and requests

Carly, Canada

Things I need from home

newspapers ✓
magazines ✓
winter coat ✓
boots ✓
diary
a small Canadian flag
apples

1 Carly and Scott are chatting online. Carly asks him to bring some more things to Japan for her. Who says each sentence? Write C (Carly) or S (Scott).

Chat

invite friends   send files   webcam

a [C] Great. And could you buy a small Canadian flag for me?

b ☐ Hi, it's me again! Can I ask you to bring some more things?

c ☐ No, sorry! I can't take apples through the airport.

d ☐ Oh, OK. One more thing. I miss the apples from home. Could you bring some apples from Canada?

e ☐ OK. Could you bring my diary? I can't find an English one here.

f ☐ No, I'm afraid not. I don't have time to go shopping.

g ☐ Yes, of course. But just small things, OK?

h ☐ Yes, OK. No problem. It's small, so I can carry it in my hand luggage.

Over to you

Imagine you live in a different country. Write an email asking a friend to bring you some things from home.

2 Put the sentences in the correct order to make the conversation between Carly and Scott.

1 [b]   2 ☐   3 ☐   4 ☐   5 ☐   6 ☐   7 ☐   8 ☐

3 Choose one expression from each box to complete the conversations. Write your answers in the correct picture.

> Can I do   Can I help   Could I have   Could you give me   Could you make
> ~~Would you like something~~

> ~~to drink?~~   some sandwiches, please?   a glass of water, please?   you, sir?
> some information, please?   something to help?

1 *Would you like something to drink?*

GRAMMAR

Present simple: positive sentences

Melek, Turkey

4 Read Melek's email to another Sofasurfer. Complete the gaps using the verbs in the box.

> has   ~~is~~   is   live   sleep   speaks

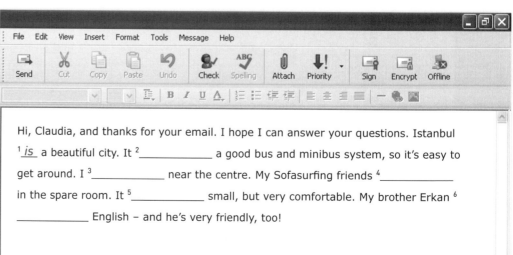

Hi, Claudia, and thanks for your email. I hope I can answer your questions. Istanbul ¹ *is* a beautiful city. It ² _____ a good bus and minibus system, so it's easy to get around. I ³ _____ near the centre. My Sofasurfing friends ⁴ _____ in the spare room. It ⁵ _____ small, but very comfortable. My brother Erkan ⁶ _____ English – and he's very friendly, too!

Interests and wants

5 Complete the Sofasurfers' posts using the words and expressions in the box.

a good job   go to   I'd like   in   ~~interested~~   learn   music   Sweden   want to

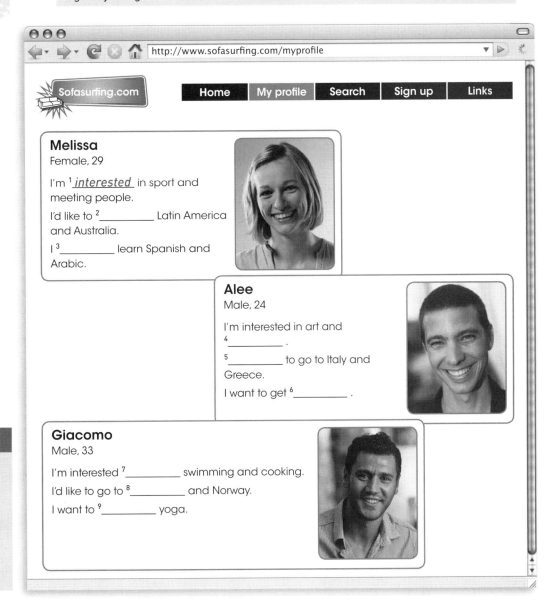

http://www.sofasurfing.com/myprofile

Sofasurfing.com   Home | My profile | Search | Sign up | Links

Melissa
Female, 29

I'm [1] _interested_ in sport and meeting people.

I'd like to [2] _____ Latin America and Australia.

I [3] _____ learn Spanish and Arabic.

Alee
Male, 24

I'm interested in art and [4] _____ .

[5] _____ to go to Italy and Greece.

I want to get [6] _____ .

Giacomo
Male, 33

I'm interested [7] _____ swimming and cooking.

I'd like to go to [8] _____ and Norway.

I want to [9] _____ yoga.

Over to you

Write four lists: things you are interested in, things you'd like to do, places you'd like to visit and things you want to learn.

TimeOut

6 Find the ten interests in the word snake.

ithyoga ous wimming ondesalsafrichess eetfootballbran umusicoacinemarro artparchitectureenfooda

1 _yoga_ _____
2 _____
3 _____
4 _____
5 _____

6 _____
7 _____
8 _____
9 _____
10 _____

EXPLOREReading

7 Look at the leaflets for English study holidays.

   a Which three countries can you study in?
   b Would you like to go to any of these countries?

A

Learn English in Ireland with Homestay English

- Live with your teacher's family
- Study one-to-one with your teacher

Flexible study courses for adults (over 18):
10–25 hours a week
2–10 weeks

Our homestay courses include visits to places of interest.
You can add activities to your course – golf, tennis and watersports are available.

Some of our teachers have specialised knowledge of subjects like medicine, marketing, graphic design, etc. We can offer English courses based on the vocabulary of these subjects.

B

Learn English in Cape Town, South Africa

Good Hope Studies was one of the first English-language schools in Cape Town, South Africa, and offers junior language courses from 14 to 16 years and adult classes from 17 plus.

You can study the following English-language courses at this school:
- standard course
- intensive course
- Cambridge Exam preparation

The courses are offered all year round. Last year, students from 50 different countries learned English at our language school.

We hope to see you here soon!

C

Study English at Bell Malta Language Centre if you want to combine language learning with watersports.

Malta is a major centre for English-language teaching. English is an official language, and people speak it everywhere on the island. Malta is the perfect choice if you want to study English while enjoying a holiday in the Mediterranean.

Bell Malta is a modern building situated in St Julian's. It is close to the beach and numerous restaurants, cafés and bars.

Top courses
English Pathways: 21 hours a week of intensive general English
Summer English: for young adults aged 16–22 years
Business English: 25 hours a week of intensive business English

Accommodation available with local families.

8 Look at Angharad's questions. Read the leaflets and check the information. Write ✓ (yes), ✗ (no) or ? (don't know) for each school.

Angharad, Switzerland

	Homestay	Good Hope	Bell School
1 Can I live with a family?	✓	?	✓
2 Can I study for an exam?			
3 Can I do an intensive course?			
4 Are there other activities (sports, etc.)?			
5 Can my 17-year-old sister do a course, too?			

Over to you

Which study holiday would you choose? Write a sentence.

9 This is the email confirmation Angharad receives for her English course. Which study holiday is it – A, B or C?

Subject: Confirmation

We are pleased to confirm your place on an intensive general English course (Ref. EP53) from 15–30 August. Your accommodation is with Mrs Vicky Ferro and family. She will contact you with more information. We look forward to welcoming you to our island.

1 Before you watch, think about these questions: Are you interested in sport? In art? Which do you prefer?

2 Watch Justyna and Laura. Circle the correct answers.

Justyna

Laura

1 Justyna is interested in art / a sport.
2 Laura is interested in art / a sport.

3 Who says these words? Write J (Justyna) or L (Laura). Watch again to check.

1 trees ☑ J
2 kayaking ☐
3 expressions ☐
4 sunny ☐
5 river ☐
6 fields ☐
7 older and younger ☐
8 bird ☐
9 cultures ☐
10 sketching ☐
11 faces ☐

kayaking   *drawing*

4 Watch again and circle the correct answers.

1 She started kayaking when she was at school / university.
2 It's very quiet / busy on the river.
3 Her favourite river is in north-east / south-west Poland.
4 There are a lot of interesting bird / animal species.
5 She thinks people are interesting / fascinating.
6 She studied anthropology / biology at university.
7 She loves painting / sketching people's faces.

5 Match the beginnings and endings of the sentences. Watch again to check.

1 **One of the things I like doing in my spare time is** ...   a ... kayaking when I was at university.
2 **I started** ...   b ... **in my spare time.**
3 **What I like about** kayaking **is** ...   c ... sketching their faces.
4 **I love** art and drawing ...   d ... **really fascinate me.**
5 People ...   e ... going kayaking.
6 **I just love** ...   f ... the variety of rivers.

6 Write about an interest you have. Try to use some of the expressions in bold in Exercise 5.

GLOSSARY

still (adjective): Something is **still** if it is not moving.
leaves (noun; singular **leaf**): The **leaves** are the small, green parts of trees.
storm (noun): bad weather, with a lot of wind and rain
banks (noun): The **bank** is the land at the sides of a river.
species /'spiːʃiːz/ (noun, singular and plural): animals or plants of the same class or type
drawing, **sketching** (nouns): making a picture with a pencil or pen

3 Your time

VOCABULARY
Free time activities

1 **Cross out the words that do *not* go with the verbs in bold.**

1 **watching** something good on TV / films / ~~the cinema~~
2 **listening to** music / a newspaper / the radio
3 **reading** jazz / a good book / a newspaper
4 **learning** new things / languages / photos
5 **playing** fishing / the drums / football
6 **going to** parties / music / the cinema
7 **talking to** my wife / my friends / languages

GRAMMAR
Present simple: negative sentences

2 **Complete the speech bubbles with *doesn't* or *don't*.**

1 I ___*don't*___ read a newspaper in the morning.

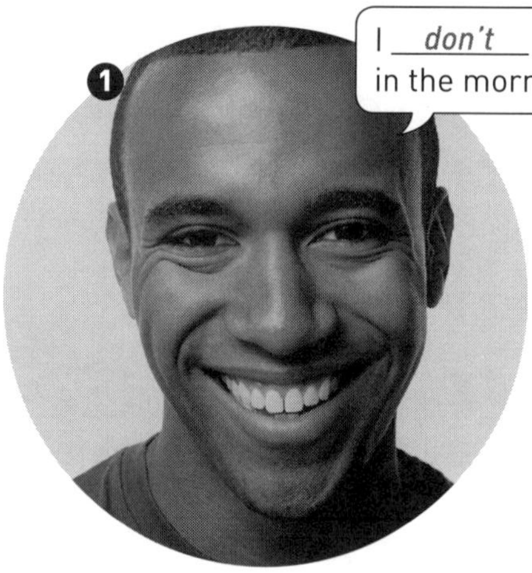

2 My parents ________ like going to parties.

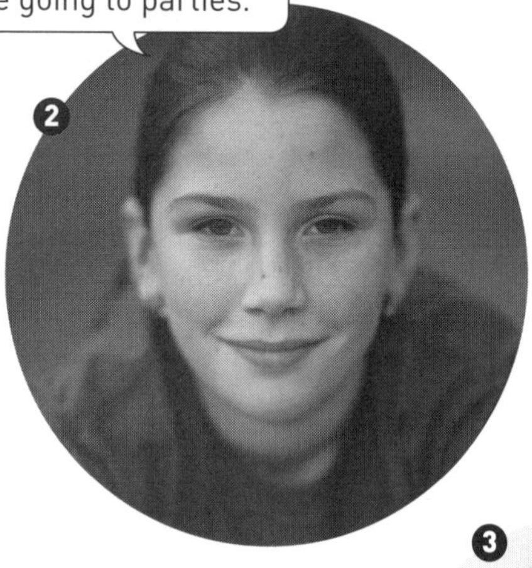

3 My brother Hans plays the piano, but he ________ play the drums.

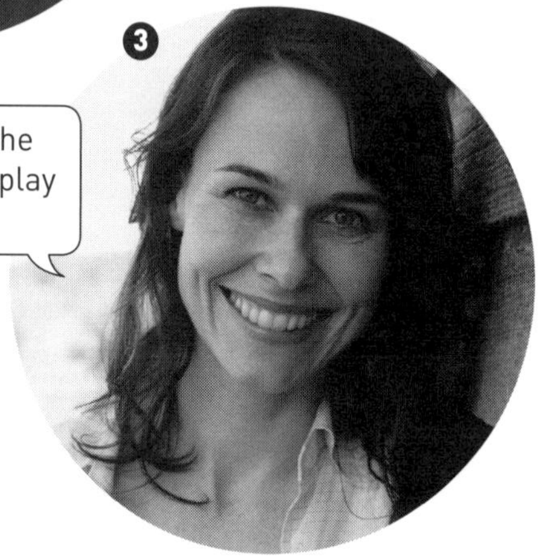

4 My sister and I ________ like watching sport on TV.

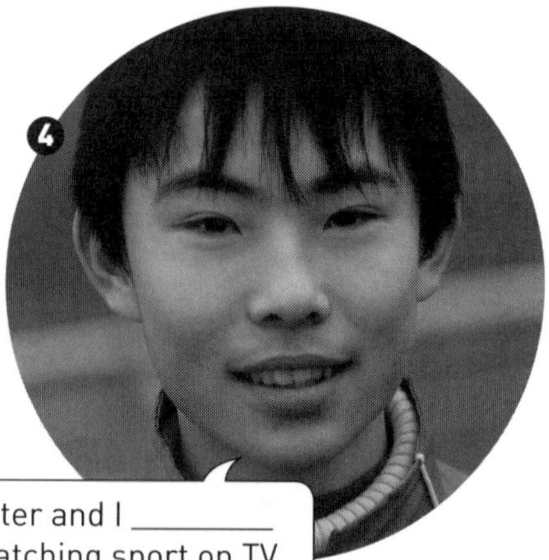

5 My English teacher ________ speak Spanish.

6 My flat ________ have a spare room.

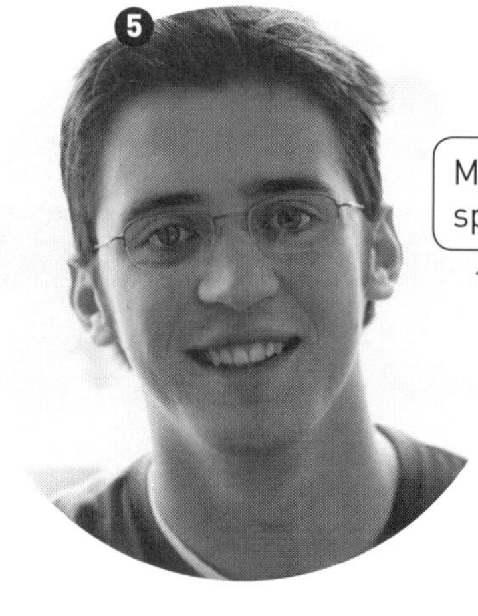

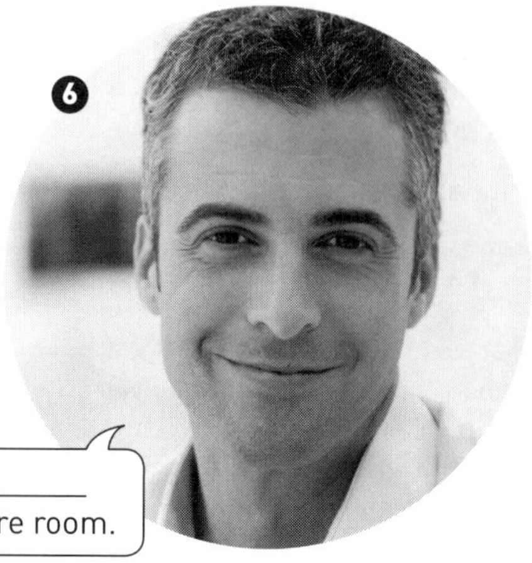

3 Look at the form that Emma has filled in and complete the sentences below.

Hobbies and interests					

Please mark how much you enjoy these things.
Circle a number between 1 and 5.
1 = I don't like it, 2 = I quite like it, 3 = I like it, 4 = I really like it, 5 = I love it

1	going to parties	①	2	3	4	5
2	watching TV	1	2	③	4	5
3	watching sport on TV	1	②	3	4	5
4	reading books	1	2	3	4	⑤
5	going to the cinema	1	2	3	④	5
6	listening to the radio	①	2	3	4	5

You say:
watch TV
      films
      something on TV
      sport on TV

1 Emma ____*doesn't like*____ going to parties.
2 She _____ watching TV.
3 Emma _____ watching sport on TV.
4 She _____ reading books.
5 Emma _____ going to the cinema.
6 She _____ listening to the radio.

Over to you

Write sentences about you, using the hobbies and interests from the form. For example, *I really like going to parties*.

VOCABULARY
Adverbs of frequency

4 Write five more sentences that are true for you. Use a word or phrase from each box.

always   usually   often   sometimes   never

have a coffee   have a shower   listen to the radio   meet friends read a newspaper   use the Internet   watch TV

in the morning   in the evening

1 *I always have a coffee in the morning.* _____
2 _____
3 _____
4 _____
5 _____
6 _____

You say:
have a bath
     a shower

GRAMMAR
Present simple: questions

5 Look at the questions about New Year in the Czech Republic. Complete them with *do* or *does*.

1 What _*do*_ you usually do for New Year?
2 _____ your friends and family come and visit you?
3 What kind of food _____ people eat?
4 _____ you play games?
5 _____ it usually snow at New Year?

6 Now match the questions from Exercise 5 (1–5) with Karel's answers (a–e).

a 　3　 We usually eat a special soup. But we don't eat chicken – it's bad luck!
b 　□　 We often go to the mountains.
c 　□　 Yes! It's very cold, too. I love snow!
d 　□　 No, we don't play any special games.
e 　□　 Sometimes. Or we all go away together.

MYEnglish

7 Read what João says and choose the correct words to complete the sentences below.

> " I come from Lisbon, but I'm a student in Coimbra. I study Economics at university, and I study English at evening classes.
> In summer, I work in a bar on the beach near Lisbon, and there are a lot of English-speaking tourists there. A lot of TV and films in Portugal are in English, too, so I watch them to help me learn.
> My English is OK, but I make some silly mistakes, for example *You like football?* instead of *Do you like football?*. People understand me, but I like to get it right. And I sometimes make mistakes with negatives, too: *I no like football* instead of *I don't like football*. I think my pronunciation is OK, usually, but my spelling in English is bad! "

João, Portugal

1 João is from Lisbon / Coimbra.
2 He studies Economics / English at university.
3 He thinks his pronunciation is OK / bad and his spelling is OK / bad.

Your English

8 Some languages don't use auxiliary verbs (like *do / does / don't / doesn't*) to make questions and negatives. What about your language?

9 Write the words in the correct order to make:

negative sentences
1 Saturdays / doesn't / He / on / work / .
   He doesn't work on Saturdays.

2 don't / children / like / homework / My / doing / .
   _____

3 like / jazz / listening / I / don't / to / .
   _____

questions
4 come / do / Where / you / from / ?
   _____

5 she / like / parties / to / Does / going / ?
   _____

6 weekends / they / at / do / do / What / ?
   _____

10 João has a problem with spelling. In Portuguese, a letter always has the same sound. In English, letters can have different sounds. What about in your language?

11 Look at these words. Cross out the four other words that are not spelled correctly and correct them.

happy

happi waching beach team meel again

night kitshen playing Inglish Friday

EXPLORE Writing

12 Look at this email invitation. Which sentence is true?

A   Victor invites Chris to the cinema on Sunday.
B   Chris invites Victor to the cinema on Sunday.

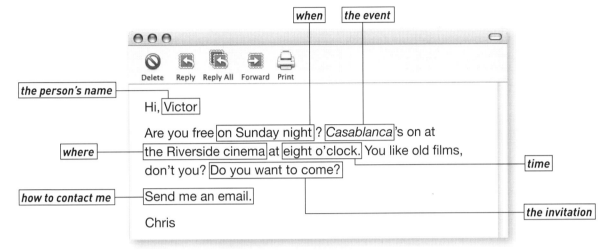

13 Now look at this email invitation. Draw lines to identify the different parts.

14 Write the expressions in the box in the correct place in the table.

> at the Golden Cow restaurant   Send me an email.   Do you want to ... ?
> I'm having a party.   ~~on Saturday~~   at our flat   Send me a text.

When	on Sunday night tonight 1 *on Saturday*
Event	Casablanca's on ... We're going for dinner ... 2
Where	at the Riverside Cinema 3 4
Invitation	Would you like to ... ? 5
How to contact me	Give me a call. 6 7

15 Think of something you would like to invite a friend to do. Write your invitation.

1 Before you watch, match the activities (1–6) with the pictures (a–f).

1 doing martial arts   c
2 playing football
3 playing computer games
4 playing the guitar
5 going to the cinema
6 watching television

2 Watch the video. Match the people with the activities in Exercise 1.

I enjoy very much cooking,
2 _____ , reading.

I like hiking, and I like ³ _____ .

I also enjoy
¹ _travelling_ .

Mainda 6

Patrizia

Adam

I love ⁴ _____
and books, and I
love ⁵ _____ .

Laura

Salvatore

Claire

I really enjoy ⁶ _____ .
I really enjoy ⁷ _____
and walking in the mountains.

3 Watch again. Complete the sentences in Exercise 2 using the phrases in the box.

computer games   eating   hiking   martial arts   reading   swimming   ~~travelling~~

4 Look at these verb patterns.

like	+ _____ing	I love reading.
love	**or**	
enjoy	+ noun	I like football.

Now look at the sentences in Exercise 3. For each one, write A (verb + _____ing) or B (verb + noun).

1 A   2 ☐   3 ☐   4 ☐☐   5 ☐☐

5 Write some sentences about yourself.

I really enjoy _____ .
I like _____ .
I love _____ .

GLOSSARY

cookery/cooking (nouns): preparing food
hiking (noun): going for long walks in the countryside
object (noun): a thing (that you can see and touch, but not a person or other living thing)
passion (noun): a strong feeling of love

Changes

GRAMMAR

Past simple verbs

1 Write the verbs in the box in the correct column (regular or irregular). Then write the past form of the irregular verbs.

| ~~buy~~ cost go have ~~like~~ listen love make meet use want work |

regular (-ed endings)

1 *like*
2 _____
3 _____
4 _____
5 _____
6 _____

irregular   **past form**

1 *buy*   → *bought*
2 _____   → _____
3 _____   → _____
4 _____   → _____
5 _____   → _____
6 _____   → _____

2 Use verbs from Exercise 1 in the past simple to complete the text about the first electric guitars. There is more than one possible answer for some of the gaps.

Electric guitars

An American company ¹___*made*___ the first electric guitars, because big jazz bands in the 1930s ²_____ to have a big guitar sound. The first designer was Harry Watson, who ³_____ for the Electro String Company, and the first guitar was the Rickenbacker. It ⁴_____ a lot of money, but many jazz musicians bought it anyway. The first record with an electric guitar appeared in 1938. A lot of musicians ⁵_____ to this new instrument and ⁶_____ the new sound. Now many types of music use electric guitars, from rock and roll to folk.

4

VOCABULARY
Past time
expressions

3 Match the expressions in the box with the numbers (1–5) on the calendar.

a couple of days ago   four days ago   ~~in March~~   last month   last week

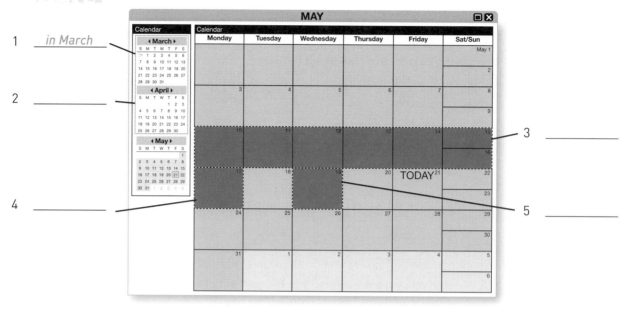

1   *in March*

2   _____

3   _____

4   _____

5   _____

4 Use the calendar in Exercise 3 and write these dates in a different way.
Use expressions with *last* and *ago*. There may be more than one answer.

1   May 14th   *last Friday / a week ago* _____
2   March   _____
3   April 30th   _____
4   January   _____
5   May 18th   _____

5 Complete the sentences so they are true for you.

I bought a new mobile phone last week.

1   _____ last week.
2   _____ last month.
3   _____ two weeks ago.
4   _____ in 2008.
5   _____ a couple of days ago.

VOCABULARY
Things for a trip

6 Complete the words with the vowels: *a, e, i, o, u*.

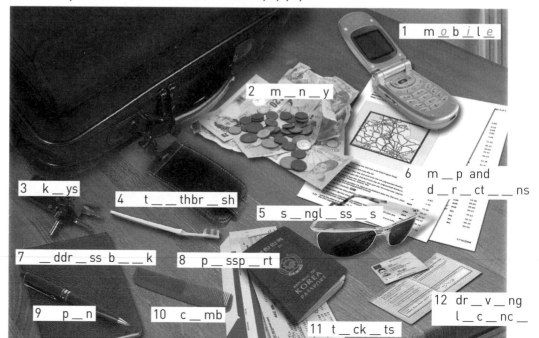

1 m _o_ b _i_ l _e_
2 m _ _ n _ y
3 k _ ys
4 t _ _ thbr _ sh
5 s _ ngl _ ss _ s
6 m _ p and d _ r _ ct _ _ ns
7 _ ddr _ ss b _ _ k
8 p _ ssp _ rt
9 p _ n
10 c _ mb
11 t _ ck _ ts
12 dr _ v _ ng l _ c _ nc _

Over to you

When is your next
trip? Make a list of
things to take.

20

Onyinye

GRAMMAR
Past simple

7 Onyinye's family moved from Nigeria to Scotland. Complete the questions using the words in the box.

| Did did did have How she she What ~~When~~ |

1 ___When___ did Onyinye's family move to Scotland?
2 Did _____ _____ a lot of memories of Nigeria?
3 _____ Onyinye like Scotland at first?
4 When _____ _____ see snow for the first time?
5 _____ _____ she feel when she saw the snow?
6 _____ did Onyinye and her family make in the snow?

8 Can you remember the answers to the questions? Write the number of the question from Exercise 7 next to the correct answer.

a [3] Yes, she did. It was like a holiday.
b [ ] A snowman.
c [ ] No, not really. She was very young.
d [ ] When Onyinye was five years old.
e [ ] The first winter in Scotland.
f [ ] It was a shock for her, but she had a lot of fun.

TimeOut

9 Do the technology crossword.

ACROSS

3 I bought my first _____ camera in 2006.
5 I use a PC at work, but I have a _____ at home.
7 TXT MSG = text _____

DOWN

1 I use _____ to listen to music on the bus.
2 I've got about 200 music _____ at home.
4 My _____ phone takes good photos, too.
6 I bought some music online for my MP3 _____.

EXPLORE Reading

10 Look at the newspaper article. Find the names of six songs. Which of the songs do you know?

Songs that changed my life

Music fans tell us about a song that was important in their lives

J.G. BALLARD – writer

The Teddy Bears' Picnic by Jimmy Kennedy

When I was a child in Shanghai in the 1930s, I had that record. It has all the magic of my childhood.

JEAN-PIERRE – assistant in record shop

Imagine by John Lennon

I love this song for Lennon's vision of the world. It had an enormous effect on me.

CARLOS ACOSTA – dancer

Te Doy Una Canción by Silvio Rodríguez

It's a very romantic song. When I hear it, I remember when I was a student with a group of musicians and painters in Cuba. Just guitar and voice, a very simple song.

STEVE SUTHERLAND – music journalist

Mr Tambourine Man by The Byrds

I heard this on the radio in 1965. I was nine. I didn't understand a word of it, but I knew it meant a life of freedom.

WAYNE HEMINGWAY – designer

Sunshine by Roy Ayres

It makes me happy, it makes me think of sunshine, families – nice things.

ALAIN DE BOTTON – writer

Reading, Writing and Arithmetic by The Sundays

This takes me back to the 1990s, when I left university and had a terrible time. I spent a lot of time in cafés in the sad parts of London.

11 Read the article again. Why did the people choose these songs? Tick the correct column(s) in the table.

	This song makes me think of a time in the past	I like the ideas or the feeling in this song
J.G. Ballard	✓	
Jean-Pierre		
Steve Sutherland		
Carlos Acosta		
Wayne Hemingway		
Alain de Botton		

Over to you

Do you have a song that is important for you? Why? Write one or two sentences.

1 Before you watch, do you know these technology words? Check in your dictionary.

1 DVD player   F
2 application
3 Internet
4 piece of equipment
5 computer

6 technology
7 play button
8 sound system
9 computer program

Patrizia

2 Watch Patrizia, Fred and Laura. Who says the words in Exercise 1?
Write P (Patrizia), F (Fred) or L (Laura).

3 Who talked about:

1 a child who uses a computer?
2 using a computer for work?
3 something they didn't understand at first?

4 Watch Patrizia again (00:14–00:55). Are the sentences true or false?

1 Patrizia wanted to use the Internet because her friends used it.   TRUE / FALSE
2 The first time she used it, she decided not to use it again.   TRUE / FALSE
3 The Internet is not important in her life now.   TRUE / FALSE

Fred

5 Watch Fred again (01:06–01:40). Circle the correct answers.

1 Fred is 32 / 42 years old.
2 He had his first computer when he was 10 / 12 years old.
3 His daughter is 4 / 5 years old.

6 Watch Laura again (01:41–02:13). Put the sentences in order.

☐ She did her project.
☐ She started her project again.
☐ 1 She got a new computer program.
☐ Nothing happened – the program didn't work.
☐ She had some training.

Laura

7 Which verbs in the box do Patrizia, Fred and Laura use with these phrases? Watch again to check.

> press   switch on   start   ~~use~~   use   use

1 _____use_____ the Internet
2 _____ the application
3 _____ the DVD player
4 _____ the sound system
5 _____ the play button
6 _____ the program

8 Talk about the first time you used a piece of technology, or a problem you had with it. Try to use some of these expressions from the video.

The first time I used the _____ was …

I didn't know how to …

I had my first _____ when I was …

I thought I understood everything.

Nothing happened.

GLOSSARY

amazing (adjective): very surprising, incredible
fail (verb): to not be able to do something (*I failed. = I couldn't do it.*)
the 'magic' button (noun): the button to make the program work
the mid-eighties/mid-80s (nouns): the years 1983–1987
nowadays (adverb): now, at the present time
sound system (noun): equipment to listen to music

Your space

1 _____a bridge_____

2 _____

3 _____

4 _____

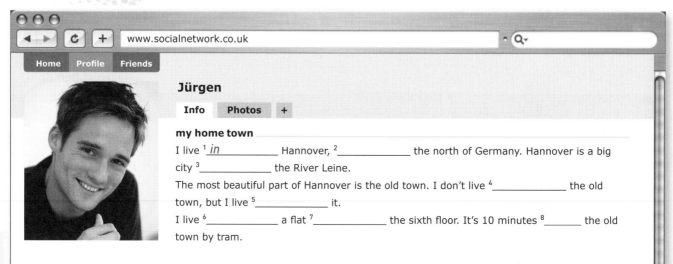

5 _____

6 _____

1 **Label the pictures using the words in the box.**

a bridge   a lake   a market   mountains   a river   a train station

2 **Complete the table with the opposites of the adjectives given.**

1	exciting	b _oring_
2	dirty	c_____
3	q_____	noisy
4	d_____	safe
5	cheap	e_____
6	b_____	ugly

3 **Complete Jürgen's text using the prepositions in the box.**

from   in   near   on

www.socialnetwork.co.uk

Home   Profile   Friends

Jürgen

Info   Photos   +

my home town

I live ¹ _in_ Hannover, ² _____ the north of Germany. Hannover is a big city ³ _____ the River Leine.

The most beautiful part of Hannover is the old town. I don't live ⁴ _____ the old town, but I live ⁵ _____ it.

I live ⁶ _____ a flat ⁷ _____ the sixth floor. It's 10 minutes ⁸ _____ the old town by tram.

GRAMMAR

There is, There are

Over to you

Write your answers to the questions in Exercise 4 for where you live.

VOCABULARY

Things in the home

4 Complete the questions with *Is* or *Are*.

1 ___Is___ there a hospital near your home?
2 _____ there a lot of parks in your town?
3 _____ there an airport in your city?
4 _____ there any mountains near where you live?
5 _____ there a river?

5 Are the sentences true or false?

1 There's a computer in the living room.　TRUE / FALSE
2 There's a washing machine in the kitchen.　TRUE / FALSE
3 There are some towels on the washing machine.　TRUE / FALSE
4 There are three wardrobes in the bedroom.　TRUE / FALSE
5 There's a bookshelf in the living room.　TRUE / FALSE

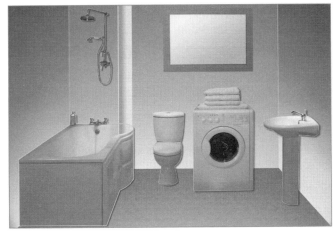

6 Write five sentences about the flat using the words in the boxes.

bathroom　bedroom　kitchen　living room

bed　cooker　fridge　shower　TV　wardrobe　washing machine　window

1 *There's a bed in the bedroom.*
2 _____
3 _____
4 _____
5 _____

Over to you

Write five true sentences about the house or flat that you live in.

MYEnglish

7 Read the text. Are the sentences true or false?

1 Jürgen speaks English every day at work.   TRUE / FALSE
2 Ute studies English at university.   TRUE / FALSE
3 German prepositions are always the same as English prepositions.   TRUE / FALSE

Jürgen, Germany

Ute, Germany

> " I come from Hannover in the north of Germany. I work for an advertising company,
> and we do a lot of business with international companies – all in English! I studied
> English at school and I use it every day for work, so I think my English is OK. My
> colleague, Ute, doesn't speak English very often, but she is taking English lessons
> after work at a language school. Sometimes she asks me to help her. She sometimes
> makes mistakes because she thinks in German – so she says 'there gives' instead of
> 'there is' because that's what we say in German. Or she makes preposition mistakes
> like 'at Monday' instead of 'on Monday' because in German we use the same
> preposition for both. She makes mistakes, but I think she speaks English very well! "

Your English

8 Sometimes people make mistakes because they try to translate from their own language.
Do you do this in your language?

9 Ute has problems with these types of sentences in English. Circle the correct words.

1 There (is) / gives a plant in the kitchen.
2 Say / Tell hello to him from me.
3 It / There is a man in the garden.
4 Where is my watch? Can you see her / it?
5 There is / are some problems with the air conditioning today.

10 Ute also makes mistakes with prepositions. Choose the correct prepositions.

1 I don't work at / (on) Saturdays.
2 The bus stop is before / in front of our house.
3 He is a student in / to London.
4 Look at this photo of / from my sister. She's the one with short hair.
5 I'm reading a book from / by John Steinbeck.

11 Do you help any friends or colleagues with English? What mistakes do they make?
How do you help?

EXPLOREWriting

You say:
flat-sit
house-sit

12 Stella is flat-sitting for a friend in Barcelona, Spain. Read the first part of her postcard to her friend in New Zealand. <u>Underline</u> the adjectives.

> Hi Louise!
> Hello from Barcelona!
> I really love it here. I live in the centre of the city. It's very noisy, but the buildings are beautiful, and everything is so exciting. It's a bit expensive, but that's not a problem - yet!
>
> Louise Walker

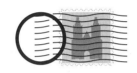

13 Complete the second part of Stella's postcard using the words in the box.

> bedroom   chairs   cooker   ~~living room~~   shelves   wardrobe

> The flat is great. It has a small ¹ <u>living room</u> with a sofa, and a table with two ²_____.
> The kitchen is really small, too, but it has a ³_____ and a fridge. The ⁴_____ is great: there's a bed, some ⁵_____ and a ⁶_____. It's a small flat, but I think it's perfect.
> I promise to email soon!
> Love Stella

14 Imagine you are looking after a friend's flat in a different city. Circle the adjectives that describe the new city.

> beautiful   boring   cheap   clean   dangerous   dirty
> exciting   expensive   noisy   quiet   safe   ugly

15 What is your new flat like? What is in it? Make lists.

- Rooms
- Furniture

16 Now write a postcard describing it.

1 Before you watch, think about the house or flat you live in. How would you describe it? Is it big or small? Old or new? What else can you say about it?

2 Watch Martina and Monica. Match the pictures (1–3) with the speakers. One of them talks about two places.

Martina

Monica

3 Watch again and circle the correct answers.

1 Martina's favourite room was in Germany / Italy.
2 It was a small / big room.
3 She liked / didn't like the city she lived in.
4 Monica liked the house in Italy / France.
5 In France, she lived in an apartment / a house.
6 She liked / didn't like the place in France as much as the place in Italy.

4 Complete the text about Martina's favourite room using the words in the box.

> had   liked   ~~lived~~   lived   was

My favourite room is the room I ^{1}___*lived*___ in in Germany. It ^{2}_____ a high ceiling and a beautiful wooden floor. It ^{3}_____ quite large. I ^{4}_____ with really nice people and I really ^{5}_____ the room and the city.

5 Match the adjectives (1–6) with what they describe (a–f). Watch again to check.

1 very high   a people
2 really beautiful wooden   b city
3 really nice   c ceiling
4 big   d house
5 tranquil, calm, beautiful   e wallpaper
6 patterned   f floor

6 Write about your favourite house or flat. Think back to what you said in Exercise 1.

GLOSSARY

calm (adjective): peaceful and quiet
ceiling (noun): When you are indoors, the **ceiling** is what you see above your head.
floor (noun): When you are indoors, the **floor** is under your feet.
patterned (adjective): The room in picture 3 above has **patterned** wallpaper.
tranquil (adjective): peaceful; without noise
wallpaper (noun): paper used to cover the walls of a room

What would you like?

VOCABULARY
Shops and shopping

1 Magda works at the information desk in a shopping centre. Complete her answers to the visitors' questions using the words in the box.

> a cash machine ~~a clothes shop~~ the computer shop
> an escalator the pharmacy The toilets

Excuse me, I want to buy a pair of jeans.

Yes, there's [1] *a clothes shop* upstairs.

Where can I get money here?

There's [2]_____ at the bank.

Hello, where can I wash my hands, please?

Where can I buy some headphones for my computer?

[3]_____ are over there, near the exit.

At [4]_____, TechLand.

Hello, how do I get upstairs?

Can I buy medicine here?

Well, there's [5]_____ or a lift.

Yes, at [6]_____.

VOCABULARY
Buying things

2 Complete the shopping expressions with *How much* or *How many*.

1 _____ is this one?

2 _____ packets would you like?

3 _____ CDs are there in the pack?

4 _____ do these jeans cost?

3 Match the answers (a–d) with the questions (1–4) in Exercise 2.

a ☐ It's $3, or the big one is $5.50.
b ☐ They're £39.95.
c ☐ Ten, or we have packs of 25, too.
d ☐ Just one, please.

4 Who says what? Write C (customer) or A (shop assistant).

1 [C] How much are ...
2 ☐ I'd like ...
3 ☐ How many would you like?
4 ☐ ... anything else?
5 ☐ Can I help you?
6 ☐ I'll have ...

5 Complete the conversation with the expressions in Exercise 4.

ASSISTANT [1] *Can I help you* ?

CUSTOMER Yes, [2]_____ some headphones for my computer.

ASSISTANT Well, the headphones are over here. These are quite basic, but they're fine.

CUSTOMER [3]_____ they?

ASSISTANT €12.95.

CUSTOMER OK. I'll take them.

ASSISTANT Do you want [4]_____?

CUSTOMER Yes, I need some CDs, too.

ASSISTANT [5]_____? They're in packets of 10.

CUSTOMER [6]_____ 10, thanks.

6 Complete the food words with vowels: *a, e, i, o, u*.

1 ch _i_ ck _e_ n
2 s __ lm __ n
3 s __ __ s __ g __ s
4 y __ gh __ rt
5 c __ rr __ ts

6 __ l __ v __ s
7 __ n __ __ ns
8 br __ __ d
9 ch __ __ s __
10 r __ c __

7 Match the words from Exercise 6 (1–10) with the pictures (a–j).

8 (Circle) the correct words.

1 Bananas and lemons (have a skin) / are round.
2 Apples and oranges are not very good for you / round.
3 Potatoes and pasta are high in carbohydrates / have a skin.
4 Broccoli and lettuce are good if you're on a diet / sweet.
5 Chocolate and butter are round / not very good for you.

9 Complete the table using the words in the box.

a   a lot of   an   ~~many~~   much   pasta   some   strawberries

Countable	Uncountable
How ¹ _many_ eggs do you want?	How ² _____ chocolate do you eat?
I'd like ³ _____ apple, ⁴ _____ watermelon and some ⁵ _____ , please.	Do you want ⁶ _____ bread?
I eat ⁷ _____ potatoes.	I eat a lot of ⁸ _____ .

10 Complete what Belén says about what she eats and drinks using the words in the box.

a   a lot of   five   How much   ~~some~~

Belén, Spain

My diet? Well, I don't eat meat very often, and I try to have at least
¹ _some_ fresh fruit and vegetables every day, and rice or pasta. I have
² _____ sandwich for lunch, and I normally eat at home in the evening.
³ _____ coffee do I drink? Well, I admit I drink ⁴ _____ coffee.
I know it's bad for you, but I have about ⁵ _____ cups a day!

Time Out

11 Find 11 more food words.

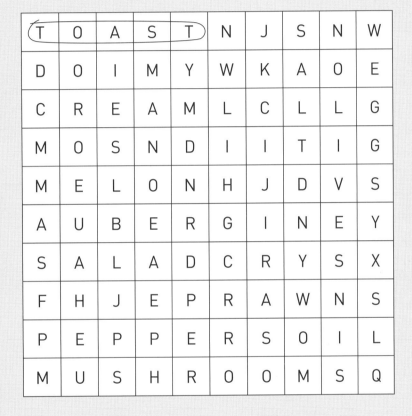

T	O	A	S	T	N	J	S	N	W
D	O	I	M	Y	W	K	A	O	E
C	R	E	A	M	L	C	L	L	G
M	O	S	N	D	I	I	T	I	G
M	E	L	O	N	H	J	D	V	S
A	U	B	E	R	G	I	N	E	Y
S	A	L	A	D	C	R	Y	S	X
F	H	J	E	P	R	A	W	N	S
P	E	P	P	E	R	S	O	I	L
M	U	S	H	R	O	O	M	S	Q

EXPLORE Reading

12 Look at the takeaway menu below. Are the sentences true or false?

1 You can order food from Mae's Place on the Internet.   TRUE / FALSE
2 You can order food 24 hours a day.   TRUE / FALSE
3 Mae's Place can deliver food to you at work.   TRUE / FALSE
4 You can ask for food that isn't on the menu.   TRUE / FALSE

Open 12 pm – 2 am every day

Takeaway menu

To place your order, call **3392704**.
Your takeaway is ready for collection in 15 minutes.

Too busy to leave work?

We have the answer! If you can't come to Mae's Place, we can bring Mae's Place to you!

We can arrange special requests for food and drink. Please allow at least 48 hours.

For more information, call us on 3392704.

Sandwiches

Roast beef with mild mustard	€6
Roast lamb with hummus and salad	€6
Cheese and tomato	€4.50
Cream cheese with smoked salmon	€7.50

Greek sandwich: feta cheese, lettuce, olives, cucumber and tomato	€5.50
Egg mayonnaise	€4.50
Chicken salad	€6
Cajun chicken with grilled peppers and spicy mayonnaise	€6
Chinese spicy prawns with salad	€6.50
Tuna and spring onion with mayonnaise	€4.50

Desserts

Fresh fruit salad with yoghurt	€3.50
Apple pie with cream	€4.50

Drinks

Bottled water	€2
Fresh fruit juices	€3.50

13 Do you know the food adjectives in the menu? Match the adjectives (1–6) with the correct meanings (a–f). Use a dictionary if necessary.

1 bottled   a cooked with oil in the oven
2 fresh   b cooked under the grill or on a barbecue
3 roast   c not very strong
4 mild   d in a bottle
5 grilled   e with a lot of spices
6 spicy   f natural, not frozen or in a packet

14 Cross out the words which do *not* go with the adjectives in bold.

1 **roast**   lamb / beef / mayonnaise
2 **fresh**   fish / mustard / fruit
3 **bottled**   fish / water / juice
4 **grilled**   fish / chicken / salad

Over to you

Choose something to eat and drink. Tick (✓) the menu.

15 Choose a sandwich from the menu for each of these people.

1 I don't eat meat, chicken, fish or cheese.
2 I'd like a chicken sandwich, but nothing spicy.
3 Can I have a sandwich with fish or seafood? No mayonnaise or cheese, please.
4 I like meat, but I'd rather not have vegetables or salad in my sandwich.

1 Before you watch, do you know any typical food from Poland, Syria or Italy?

2 Watch Adam, Mouhammad and Laura. Match the names (1–3) with the topics (a–c).

Adam

Mouhammad

Laura

1 Adam (from Poland)
2 Mouhammad (from Syria)
3 Laura (from Italy)

a different types of food in his/her country
b something he/she enjoys cooking
c a typical dish from his/her country

3 Watch again and circle the correct answers.

1 Adam likes / doesn't like eating pierogi.
2 He can / can't cook pierogi.
3 Which adjective does Mouhammad *not* use to describe Syrian cuisine?
   Greek / Turkish / Italian / Mediterranean / French / Syrian
4 Laura can / can't make pasta.
5 She makes / doesn't make vegetarian lasagne.

4 Complete the sentences using the food words in the box. Watch again to help you.

cheese ~~dumpling~~ fillings lasagne meat mushroom
onion pasta potatoes spices vegetables

Pierogi are a kind of [1] _dumpling_ . They can have different [2]_____ .
A popular one is [3]_____ , [4]_____ and a bit of [5]_____ .

Syrian dishes contain [6]_____ , different types of [7]_____ , all
together with special [8]_____ .

Laura's favourite thing is making [9]_____ , especially [10]_____ .
Her favourite is the [11]_____ one.

pierogi

lasagne

5 Describe the cuisine or a typical dish from your country.

GLOSSARY

cuisine /kwɪˈziːn/ (noun): The **cuisine** of a country is its typical style of cooking.
dish (noun): food prepared in a particular way. A **dish** is also a type of plate.
dumpling (noun): round ball made with flour and cooked in water
filling (noun): The **filling** is the part in the middle of food like a sandwich, a cake, etc.
recipe /ˈresɪpiː/ (noun): the instructions for making a particular dish
spices (plural noun): A **spice** is a powder made from part of a plant, e.g. pepper, chilli.
vegetarian (noun and adjective): A **vegetarian** is a person who doesn't eat meat. **Vegetarian** food doesn't contain meat.

Work-life balance

VOCABULARY

Work and studies

1 Elsa

2 Raymond

3 Nikos

4 Beth

5 Mathias

6 Sangeeta

1 Complete the names of the jobs.

1 a _c c o u n t a n_ t

2 a _ _ _ _ _ _ _ _ _ t

3 d _ _ _ _ _ r

4 e _ _ _ _ _ _ _ _ r

5 m _ _ _ _ _ _ _ n

6 j _ _ _ _ _ _ _ _ _ _ t

2 What did each person study?

1 Elsa studied _a c c o u n t i n g_ at university.

2 Raymond studied _ _ _ _ _ _ _ _ _ _ _ _ _ _ at college.

3 Nikos studied _ _ _ _ _ _ _ _ _ _ for seven years.

4 Beth did an _ _ _ _ _ _ _ _ _ _ _ _ _ course.

5 Mathias went to _ _ _ _ _ _ school.

6 Sangeeta studied _ _ _ _ _ _ _ _ _ _ _ _ .

VOCABULARY

spend

3 Write five more sentences about *your* typical day using an expression in each box (or an expression / activity of your own).

| 45 minutes | two hours | a lot of time | eight hours |

| travelling to and from work/college | sleeping | watching TV with friends |

1 _I spend two hours a day travelling to and from work._

2 _____

3 _____

4 _____

5 _____

6 _____

GRAMMAR

Present progressive: talking about now

4 Complete the sentences using *is*, *isn't*, *are* or *aren't*.

1 Jan ___*is*___ working in the kitchen this morning. ✓
2 María and Pilar _____ working today. ✗
3 Tibor and Eva _____ having a meal with friends. ✓
4 Danny _____ studying at the moment – he's at the gym. ✗
5 Fatima _____ travelling home from work. ✓
6 Svetlana _____ relaxing at home – she has a lot of work to do. ✗

5 Circle the correct forms of the verbs to complete the sentences.

1 Jan usually works / is working in the evening, but this month, he works / is working in the morning.
2 It's Friday and María and Pilar don't work / aren't working on Saturdays, so they watch / are watching a late film this evening.
3 Tibor and Eva often go / are going to restaurants with friends. Tonight they have / are having an Italian meal.
4 Danny does / is doing weight-training at the gym this morning. He goes / is going to the gym twice a week.
5 Fatima sits / is sitting on the train at the moment. She spends / is spending an hour on the train every evening.
6 Svetlana has an important job. She works / is working for a big company. At the moment, she writes / is writing a report at home.

VOCABULARY

Saying you're busy

6 Complete the conversations using the expressions in the box.

> not interested   in the middle of dinner   not feeling well
> ~~watching a film~~   working on a report

Sorry, but I'm *watching a film*.

Do you want to play cards with me?

Can you talk at the moment?

Well, actually, I'm _____.

Do you want to come out with us?

Sorry, I'm _____.

Can I tell you about—?

Sorry, I'm _____.

Can you look at this for me?

Well, actually, I'm _____ at the moment.

MYEnglish

7 Read the text. Are the sentences true or false?

Sara, Argentina

"I love living and working in London. It's a fantastic city, and it's very good practice for my English. At the museum where I work, I speak English with people from all over the world – it's really interesting. My English is quite good now, because I speak English all the time. I can understand most things that people *say*, but sometimes I don't understand how British people *act*. I think people say 'please' and 'thank you' more here than in Argentina. I don't always know when to say 'please' or 'excuse me' or 'sorry'. People say 'sorry' a lot here! And I don't know when to kiss my English friends to say hello. I always kiss my friends in Argentina when we meet."

1 Sara works in London.   TRUE / FALSE
2 Sara only speaks English to British people.   TRUE / FALSE
3 Sara thinks people often say 'sorry' in Britain. TRUE / FALSE

Your English

8 Sara speaks English very well, but isn't always sure how to act or what to say in Britain. What about you? Do people say 'please' or 'sorry' a lot in your country?

9 Look at these pictures and write what you would say in your language in each situation.

You stand on someone's toe.

You want a coffee.

You don't hear what someone says.

10 Now match these sentences to the pictures in Exercise 9.

a Could I have a coffee, please? ☐
b Oh! I'm very sorry.   ☐
c Sorry?   ☐

11 Do you say the same thing in your language, or is it different?

EXPLORE Writing

12 Read Sara's blog entry. Do you think Sara has a good work-life balance?

BlogSpot.com:Sara

Hello from sunny London!

Posted May 19th at 2.30pm

I'm not working today, so I'm sitting in an internet café writing to all of you! I'm writing in English because I want to practise. Sorry, Juan!

This time, I'll tell you about what I do every week – so you can imagine my life here. I work at the museum from Monday to Friday, and I don't work at weekends. I go to work on the underground. It's very different from the metro in Buenos Aires! It takes an hour to get to the museum, and I work from 9 to 5.30 with an hour for lunch. The big Argentina exhibition starts next month, so we're very busy preparing for it. I'm working really hard, but I'm having a good time, too.

After work, I sometimes go out with colleagues, or I just go home. Oh – one of my new colleagues is also a guitar teacher, so I'm learning to play the guitar! I have lessons with him on Mondays and Wednesdays.

At weekends, I go sightseeing in London. There's so much to see here! But, best of all, it's summer here now – my second summer this year!

Write to me soon or read my next blog.

Besos
Sara
xxx

13 Are the sentences true or false?

1 A blog is something you write for many people to read.   TRUE / FALSE
2 Sara's blog is about her plans for the future.   TRUE / FALSE
3 Sara only uses the present simple tense.   TRUE / FALSE

14 Write the highlighted sentences in the correct column.

Things that are always true, happen all the time, or happen regularly	Things happening now or around now
I work at the museum from Monday to Friday.	*I'm not working today.*

15 Imagine you go to live and work in a new country. Write a blog post to tell your friends at home what you are doing.

a Make notes:

What are you doing at this moment? Where are you?
I'm sitting in an internet café.

What do you do every day? What time do you start work? How do you travel to work? What do you do at weekends? Where do you live?
I work from Monday to Friday.

Is anything new happening at the moment?
I'm learning to play the guitar!

b Now write your blog post.

1 Before you watch, think about this question: would you like to work from home? Why? / Why not?

2 Watch Paivi and Luis talking about working from home. Do they mention any of the same things as you?

Paivi

Luis

3 Watch again. Who finds working from home …

a easy?
b difficult sometimes?

4 Watch again and circle the correct answers.

1 Paivi / Luis grew up on a farm.
2 Paivi / Luis finds it easier to work at night.
3 Paivi / Luis is a translator.
4 Paivi / Luis has meals at fixed times.
5 Paivi / Luis thinks you need discipline to work from home.

5 Who mentions these things? Write P (Paivi), L (Luis) or B (both of them). Watch again to check.

1 having breakfast   P
2 having a cup of coffee ☐
3 having a long break   ☐
4 having lunch   ☐
5 having a deadline   ☐

6 Watch Luis again (01:15–02:13). The same two words are missing from each of these sentences. What are they?

1 You _____ _____ have discipline.
2 You _____ _____ finish.
3 You _____ _____ do your work in a certain amount of time.
4 You _____ _____ be quite disciplined.

7 Have you changed your mind about working from home? Why? / Why not?

8 Write about things you have to do in your job.

GLOSSARY

deadline (noun): a time or day by which something has to be done
discipline (noun): self-control; the ability to make yourself do what you have to do
efficient (adjective): organised and working well
grow up (verb): to go from being a child to being an adult
structure (noun): organisation; the way things are organised
temptation (noun): the desire to do or have something which you know you should not do or have

Unit 1

1 2 Nice to meet you.
   3 what's your name again?
   4 Joseph is an old friend
   5 Are you and Peter colleagues / Are Peter and you colleagues

2 2 'm 3 are 4 's 5 's 6 'm not 7 'm 8 's 9 isn't 10 's
   11 's 12 's

3 2 Virginie 3 Roland 4 Zoé 5 Odette 6 Sébastien 7 Serge
   8 André

4 2 boring 3 different every day 4 great
   5 terrible 6 difficult 7 easy 8 same every day 9 interesting

5 2 's 3 're 4 're not 5 were 6 were 7 weren't 8 was
   9 was 10 'm 11 's 12 're

6 1 False 2 True 3 True

7 2 My parents **are** teachers. 3 The boy **is** very tall.
   4 I **am** a journalist. 5 Jane and I **are** sisters.

9 1 English-speaking 2 a little

10 2, 3, 5, 7, 8

11 2 from 3 in 4 years old 5 can 6 to

DVD-ROM Extra

3 2 Poland 3 Italy 4 India 5 Istanbul in Turkey
   6 London, England

4 2 Turkish 3 Italian 4 French 5 German 6 Spanish
   7 Greek 8 Russian

5 The sentences in column A mean 'I speak this language very well.'
   The sentences in column B mean 'I speak this language a bit, not
   very well.'

Unit 2

1 b C c S d C e C f S g S h S

2 2 g 3 e 4 h 5 a 6 f 7 d 8 c

3 2 Could I have a glass of water, please?
   3 Can I help you, sir?
   4 Could you give me some information, please?
   5 Can I do something to help?
   6 Could you make some sandwiches, please?

4 2 has 3 live 4 sleep 5 is 6 speaks

5 2 go to 3 want to 4 music 5 I'd like 6 a good job 7 in
   8 Sweden 9 learn

6 2 swimming 3 salsa 4 chess 5 football 6 music 7 cinema
   8 art 9 architecture 10 food

7 a Ireland, South Africa, Malta

8
	Homestay	Good Hope	Bell School
2	?	✓	?
3	?	✓	✓
4	✓	?	✓
5	✗	✓	✓

9 C

DVD-ROM Extra

2 1 a sport 2 art

3 2 J 3 L 4 J 5 J 6 J 7 L 8 J 9 L 10 L 11 L

4 2 quiet 3 north-east 4 bird 5 fascinating 6 anthropology
   7 sketching

5 2 a 3 f 4 b 5 d 6 c

Unit 3

1 2 a newspaper (reading a newspaper)
   3 jazz (listening to jazz / playing jazz)
   4 photos (taking photos)
   5 fishing (going fishing)
   6 music (listening to music / playing music)
   7 languages (learning languages)

2 2 don't 3 doesn't 4 don't 5 doesn't 6 doesn't

3 2 likes 3 quite likes 4 loves 5 really likes 6 doesn't like

4 **Example answers**
   I never watch TV in the morning.
   I usually read a newspaper in the morning.
   I sometimes meet friends in the evening.

5 2 Do 3 do 4 Do 5 Does

6 b 1 c 5 d 4 e 2

7 1 Lisbon 2 Economics 3 OK; bad

9 2 My children don't like doing homework.
   3 I don't like listening to jazz.
   4 Where do you come from?
   5 Does she like going to parties?
   6 What do they do at weekends?

11 waching → watching   kitshen → kitchen
    meel → meal   Inglish → English

12 B

13 2 the United match / football match
    3 on Saturday
    4 Would you like to come with me?
    5 Give me a call / send me a text (on 0779 120098)

14 2 I'm having a party. 3 at the Golden Cow restaurant
    4 at our flat 5 Do you want to ...? 6 Send me an email.
    7 Send me a text.

DVD-ROM Extra

1 2 e 3 f 4 a 5 d 6 b

2 Patrizia 5 Adam 4 Laura 3 Salvatore 2 Claire 1

3 2 eating 3 swimming 4 reading
   5 computer games 6 martial arts 7 hiking

4 2 A 3 A 4 A, B 5 B, A

Unit 4

1
regular (-ed)	irregular	past form
2 listen	2 cost	cost
3 love	3 go	went
4 use	4 have	had
5 want	5 make	made
6 work	6 meet	met

2 2 wanted/liked 3 worked 4 cost 5 listened
   6 liked/loved/wanted

3 2 last month 3 last week 4 four days ago
   5 a couple of days ago

4 2 two months ago / a couple of months ago
   3 three weeks ago / last month 4 four months ago
   5 last Tuesday / three days ago

6 2 money 3 keys 4 toothbrush 5 sunglasses
   6 map and directions 7 address book 8 passport 9 pen
   10 comb 11 tickets 12 driving licence

7 2 she have 3 Did 4 did she 5 How did 6 What

8 b 6 c 2 d 1 e 4 f 5

9 **Across:** 5 laptop 7 message
   Down: 1 headphones 2 CDs 4 mobile 6 player

10 *The Teddy Bears' Picnic*; *Imagine*; *Mr Tambourine Man*; *Te Doy Una
    Canción*; *Sunshine*; *Reading, Writing and Arithmetic*

11

	This song makes me think of a time in the past	I like the ideas or the feeling in this song
J.G. Ballard	✓	
Jean-Pierre		✓
Steve Sutherland	✓	✓
Carlos Acosta	✓	
Wayne Hemingway		✓
Alain de Botton	✓	

i

DVD-ROM Extra

2 2 P 3 P 4 L 5 F 6 F 7 F 8 F 9 L
3 1 F 2 L 3 P
4 1 True 2 True 3 False
5 1 32 2 10 3 4
6 3, 5, 1, 4, 2
7 2 start (use is also possible) 3 use (switch on is also possible)
   4 switch on (use is also possible) 5 press
   6 use (start is also possible)

Unit 5

1 2 a river 3 a lake 4 mountains 5 a market 6 a train station
2 2 clean 3 quiet 4 dangerous 5 expensive 6 beautiful
3 2 in 3 on 4 in 5 near 6 in 7 on 8 from
4 2 Are 3 Is 4 Are 5 Is
5 2 False 3 True 4 False 5 True
6 **Example answers**
   There's a bed in the bedroom.
   There's a cooker in the kitchen.
   There's a fridge in the kitchen.
   There's a shower in the bathroom.
   There's a TV in the living room.
   There's a wardrobe in the bedroom.
   There's a washing machine in the kitchen.
   There's a window in the bathroom.
7 1 True 2 False 3 False
9 2 Say 3 There 4 it 5 are
10 2 in front of 3 in 4 of 5 by
12 noisy, beautiful, exciting, expensive
13 2 chairs 3 cooker 4 bedroom 5 shelves 6 wardrobe

DVD-ROM Extra

2 Martina: picture 1   Monica: pictures 2 and 3
3 2 big 3 liked 4 Italy 5 an apartment 6 didn't like
4 2 had 3 was 4 lived 5 liked
5 2 f 3 a 4 b 5 d 6 e

Unit 6

1 2 a cash machine 3 The toilets 4 the computer shop
   5 an escalator 6 the pharmacy
2 1 How much 2 How many 3 How many 4 How much
3 a 1 b 4 c 3 d 2
4 2 C 3 A 4 A 5 A 6 C
5 2 I'd like 3 How much are 4 anything else
   5 How many would you like 6 I'll have
6 2 salmon 3 sausages 4 yoghurt 5 carrots 6 olives
   7 onions 8 bread 9 cheese 10 rice
7 a 8 b 5 c 9 e 6 f 7 g 10 h 2 i 3 j 4
8 2 round 3 are high in carbohydrates
   4 good if you're on a diet 5 not very good for you
9 2 much 3 an 4 a 5 strawberries 6 some 7 a lot of
   8 pasta
10 2 a 3 How much 4 a lot of 5 five
11

T	O	A	S	T	N	J	S	N	W
D	O	I	M	Y	W	K	A	O	E
C	R	E	A	M	L	C	L	L	G
M	O	S	N	D	I	I	T	I	G
M	E	L	O	N	H	J	D	V	S
A	U	B	E	R	G	I	N	E	Y
S	A	L	A	D	C	R	Y	S	X
F	H	J	E	P	R	A	W	N	S
P	E	P	P	E	R	S	O	I	L
M	U	S	H	R	O	O	M	S	Q

12 1 False 2 False 3 True 4 True
13 2 f 3 a 4 c 5 b 6 e
14 1 mayonnaise 2 mustard 3 fish 4 salad
15 1 Egg mayonnaise 2 Chicken salad
   3 Chinese spicy prawns with salad
   4 Roast beef with mild mustard

DVD-ROM Extra

2 1 c 2 a 3 b
3 2 can't 3 French 4 can 5 makes
4 2 fillings 3 potatoes 4 cheese 5 onion 6 vegetables
   7 meat 8 spices 9 pasta 10 lasagne 11 mushroom

Unit 7

1 2 architect 3 doctor 4 engineer 5 musician 6 journalist
2 2 architecture 3 medicine 4 engineering 5 music
   6 journalism
3 **Example answers**
   I spend eight hours a day sleeping.
   I spend a lot of time watching TV.
   I don't spend a lot of time with friends.
   I spend two hours on the Internet.
   I spend half an hour on the train every day.
4 2 aren't 3 are 4 isn't 5 is 6 isn't
5 2 don't work; are watching 3 go; are having 4 is doing; goes
   5 is sitting; spends 6 works; is writing
6 2 in the middle of dinner 3 not feeling well 4 not interested
   5 working on a report
7 1 True 2 False 3 True
10 a 2 b 1 c 3
13 1 True
   2 False (Sara's blog is about her life in London at the moment.)
   3 False (Sara uses the present simple and present progressive.)
14

Things that are always true, happen all the time, or happen regularly	Things happening now or around now
I don't work at weekends. I go to work on the underground. It takes an hour to get to the museum I work from 9 to 5.30 with an hour for lunch. After work, I sometimes go out with colleagues I just go home. I have lessons with him on Mondays and Wednesdays. At weekends, I go sightseeing in London.	I'm sitting in an internet café I'm writing in English because I want to practise. I'm working really hard I'm having a good time I'm learning to play the guitar!

DVD-ROM Extra

3 a easy: Paivi b difficult sometimes: Luis
4 1 Paivi 2 Luis 3 Paivi 4 Paivi 5 Luis
5 2 B 3 L 4 P 5 L
6 have to

Unit 8

1 2 twins 3 dad 4 mum 5 grandfather 6 grandmother
   7 children 8 aunt 9 nephew 10 niece
2 2 funny 3 hard-working 4 creative 5 adventurous
3 2 pale 3 hair 4 brown 5 wearing 6 jacket
4 2 've got 3 Have you got 4 haven't got 5 hasn't got 6 Has
5 2 's got 3 hasn't got 4 hasn't got 5 have; got
6 2 get 3 talk 4 get 5 like 6 spend 7 know 8 are
7 2 C 3 C 4 NC 5 C 6 C 7 NC 8 C
8 wife, cousin, son, grandmother, dad, parents, uncle, twin(s),
   children, niece, mum, nephew, grandfather, husband, daughter

9 1 False 2 False 3 True
10 2 a 3 b 4 c 5 d
11 1 designer 2 rock and folk 3 surfing 4 cold

DVD-ROM Extra

3 1 Nilgun 2 Leo 3 Hitin
4 2 His sisters give him 3 look 4 knows 5 two years 6 phone
5 2 love 3 close 4 young 5 call; make sure 6 visit
7 in touch 8 mum and dad

Unit 9

1 2 I cycle 3 I get a taxi 4 I drive 5 I get the bus
6 I ride a motorbike
2 2 do you know 3 best way 4 near here 5 take
3 2 What's the best way to get there? 3 Is it far?
4 How long does it take to walk?
5 And do you know what time it opens?
4 2 busier 3 more dangerous 4 the quickest
5 more interesting 6 the easiest
6 2 Departure 3 From 4 Direct 5 Price
7 1 Excuse me, how long does it take to get to London?
2 And how much does an open return cost, please?
3 OK, and is it direct?
4 What time does the next train leave?
8 1 False 2 True 3 True
10 2 slowly 3 dangerous 4 busy 5 expensive
12 2 a 3 c 4 b 5 a 6 b
13 Map A
14 1 The bus stop (Bus 128) is nearer
It's easier to come by bus or metro.
2 The nearest metro station is Priory Road.
The nearest car park is in Smithfield Street.

DVD-ROM Extra

2 learning English, dolphins, kangaroos, pizza, Sydney, trucks
3 1 18 2 France 3 years 4 couldn't understand anything
5 months
4 Picture 1
5 4, 2, 5, 1, 3
6 1 c 2 a 3 b

Unit 10

1 2 funny; laugh 3 scary; horrible 4 serious 5 love
6 an exciting; a lot 7 real 8 future
2 2 We could get 3 That sounds good 4 I'm not sure
5 Why don't we rent a DVD 6 Fine with me
3 2 are/'re coming 3 am/'m flying 4 are/'re going
5 is/'s arriving 6 am/'m coming back
7 are/'re waiting 8 isn't/is not working
4 2 F 3 F 4 F 5 N 6 F 7 N 8 N
5 2 – 3 – 4 on 5 – 6 – 7 at 8 in
6 2 ✓ 3 ✓ 4 She's speaking to Giulia on Friday morning. 5 ✓
6 ✓ 7 She's going to the cinema (with Paul) on Friday evening.
8 She's meeting Zhen at the airport on Saturday.
7 2 directed by 3 set in 4 it's about 5 character 6 stars
7 funny
8 See answers on page 57.
9 Classical music, Film, Children's events, Jazz, Walks, Rock music
10 1 False 2 True 3 True 4 False
11 1 Scandellara Festival (Jurassic Rock) 2 City Walks
3 Kids' Summer (Clowns) 4 Open-air jazz

DVD-ROM Extra

2 2 H 3 A 4 A 5 H
3 1 b 2 a 3 b
4 2 fun 3 love story 4 happy 5 songs 6 family 7 friends
5 1 d 2 c 3 b 4 a

Unit 11

1 2 check in 3 boarding gate 4 baggage drop
5 baggage reclaim 6 customs 7 passport control
2 2 belt 3 passport 4 pack 5 laptop 6 gate 7 keys 8 bag
9 anything
3 2 S 3 C 4 C 5 S 6 C 7 S 8 S 9 C
4 a 3 b 2 c 5 d 1 e 4
5 a 2,8 b 3, 10 c 4,7 d 1 e 6,9 f 5
6 2 at the time 3 the south of 4 I was with 5 and then
6 in the middle of 7 In the end 8 It was quite frightening
7 2 waited 3 shopping 4 checked 5 cancelled 6 wanted
7 delayed 8 started 9 checked 10 delayed
8 1 a little 2 reading
9 4, 5, 8
11 2 understand 3 spell 4 how much
5 slow down 6 which
12 2 the travel company 3 Greece 4 delayed
5 an apology and some money
13 a 3 b 1 c 2
14 2 free seats 3 to complain 4 to receive 5 was delayed
6 satisfied 7 some compensation
15 1 Dear Sir or Madam 2 I am writing to …
3 I look forward to your reply 4 Yours faithfully

DVD-ROM Extra

2 Croatia and the USA
3 2 similar 3 meaning 4 some trousers 5 'year' 6 helicopter
7 front 8 glass 9 a couple of hours
4 1 excited; confident 2 offended 3 amazing

Unit 12

1 2 throat 3 mouth 4 back 5 arm 6 elbow 7 wrist
8 shoulder 9 finger 10 leg 11 knee 12 ankle
2 2 sore throat 3 every four to six hours 4 children under 12
5 WARNING! 6 allergic to 7 Keep away from
3 2 should (G) 3 should (L) 4 Get (L) 5 should (G) 6 Take (G)
7 shouldn't (L) 8 Don't listen (G)
5 2 a 3 d 4 b 5 e 6 c
6 have a meeting, have a party, have fun, have lunch
take a train, take tablets
spend money, spend time
7 2 take a train 3 have fun 4 have a meeting 5 spend; time
8

L	Q	Z	E	W	Y	W	T	U	S	P	I	G	S	M
Y	K	Y	U	B	F	U	H	R	S	N	A	D	Q	D
E	T	I	V	O	Z	T	R	U	M	K	Z	L	T	Q
N	E	C	K	H	N	O	O	Z	F	C	I	R	L	N
C	S	V	I	E	Q	E	A	E	U	T	L	N	J	U
C	T	M	Y	A	B	G	T	K	U	S	A	B	K	T
T	O	U	G	D	Y	Z	Y	Z	N	E	E	A	O	F
F	M	S	P	O	V	P	Q	N	I	E	W	C	D	A
D	A	C	B	U	O	K	S	X	M	S	E	K	K	C
T	C	L	H	E	S	Y	R	F	I	N	G	E	R	E
G	H	E	E	A	N	K	L	E	W	J	R	A	P	F
F	U	F	H	J	L	S	M	V	X	H	E	Z	S	N
G	L	B	N	M	U	F	O	O	T	V	Y	K	V	X
Y	J	E	M	O	U	T	H	I	L	M	L	C	L	O
I	Q	M	G	P	C	H	S	H	O	U	L	D	E	R

9 A 1 B 3 C 2
10 4 a 8 c 12 b
11 b 8 c 11 d 10 e 5 f 1
12 b ✗ c ✓ d ✗ e ✗ f ✓

DVD-ROM Extra

2 1 sleep 2 exercise 3 food and diet 4 medicine
3 2 boring 3 a couple of times 4 brown; wholemeal
5 buys organic food 6 Ayurvedic
4 1 b iii 2 c ii 3 a i
5 2 a 3 d 4 f 5 b

Unit 13

1 2 i 3 b 4 l 5 d, (f) 6 j 7 k 8 a 9 e/j/l 10 b/c/i/l
11 a/f/g/i 12 b/h/i/l
2

	Verb	Past participle
Regular verbs (–ed)	use	used
	smoke	smoked
	play	played
	work	worked
	like	liked
	want	wanted
Irregular	meet	met
	eat	eaten
	be	been
	read	read
	have	had
	see	seen

3 2 city walls 3 palace 4 sculpture 5 ruins 6 waterfall
7 tomb 8 fountain 9 statue 10 museum
4 1 wanted 2 seen 3 eaten 4 met
5 2 a 3 e 4 c 5 f 6 b
6 2 Have you (ever) been to New York?
Yes, it's a fantastic city.
3 Have you (ever) eaten Thai curry?
No, I haven't. I don't really like spicy food.
4 Have you (ever) seen the Pyramids in Cairo?
Yes, they're incredible!
5 Have you (ever) been to France?
Yes, but I've only been to Paris. What's the rest of
the country like?
6 Have you (ever) heard of Uluru National Park?
Yes, I have, but I've never been there.
7 1 In the international department of a bank in The Hague.
2 He has a lot of colleagues who are not from his country.
3 He finds it hard to pronounce the *th* sound. He uses the present
perfect instead of the past simple.
11 2 P 3 M/P 4 P 5 M/P 6 M
12 1 one of the 2 biggest 3 best place
13 2 There 3 has 4 is 5 There
14 1 in 2 on; of 3 past 4 from; in
15 1 objects from Africa, Asia and Peru
2 The park has a café, a children's play area and a small lake.

DVD-ROM Extra

2 a
3 working with local colleagues, sharing professional skills, cultural
experiences, an insight into working abroad
4 1 Africa 2 marketing and communication
3 a holiday 4 really enjoyed
5 2 in 3 abroad 4 for 5 in 6 in 7 in

Unit 14

2 2 too much 3 enough 4 enough 5 too much 6 not enough
7 enough 8 enough 9 too much
3 2 got 3 got 4 had 5 ate 6 got 7 took up 8 went 9 had
10 moved 11 started
4 2 I'm going **to** study in the States for six months.
3 I'm hoping **to** get married in the future.
4 I'**d / would** like to take up a new sport …
5 I'**m / am** going to start a new job next month.
6 I'd like **to** have children in the future.
5 1 Gemma 2 Anne-Marie
6 2 Where would you like to go to?
3 I think it's too busy
4 accommodation is really expensive.
5 looks good to me
6 I'd like to do some sightseeing
7 1 F (They are the first letters of the months of the year.)
2 They are the same: $\frac{1}{8}$
3 BANANA (You cross out S-I-X L-E-T-T-E-R-S!)
4 They are both in the middle of waTer.
5 a stamp (It stays in the corner of the letter.)
6 CARROT, ONION, LETTUCE, POTATO, BROCCOLI (They are all
vegetables.)
7 Two legs and two eyes – we didn't ask about the spiders!
8 CapriCORn and SCORpio
9 First mistake: the correct spelling is *senten**c**e*.
Second mistake: the sentence only has one mistake, not two!
10 All of them!
8 2 E 3 A 4 A, B, D 5 D, F 6 C, E
9 2 False 3 True 4 False 5 True 6 False
10 1 B 2 D 3 F 4 C
11 Holiday E
12 a 4 b 1 c 3 d 2
13 Holiday F

DVD-ROM Extra

1 1 b 2 c 3 a
2 1 S 2 L 3 M
3 a) health, child care, work
b) getting information for the programme, structuring the
programme, working with sound, asking good questions
4 1 has always wanted 2 exciting 3 jump with an instructor
5 2 training 3 university 4 learned 5 classroom
6 opportunities 7 teach
6 1 b 2 c 3 a 4 d

8 What's she like?

VOCABULARY
Family

1 Complete what Aziza says about her family using the words in the box.

> aunt ~~brothers~~ children dad grandfather
> grandmother mum nephew niece twins

Aziza, Lebanon

I have two ¹ _brothers_ – George and Hani – and a sister, Camille. She was born 20 minutes before me, so obviously, we're ² _____! My ³ _____, Elias, is a police officer, and my ⁴ _____, Mariam, looks after the house. My ⁵ _____ and ⁶ _____, Khaled and Amira, live with us, too. George and Hani go to school, and I'm a student at the university, but Camille is married and has two little ⁷ _____, so I'm an ⁸ _____! My ⁹ _____, Karim, is three years old, and my ¹⁰ _____, Maha, is just four months old.

Khaled   Amira

Mariam   Elias

Sami   Camille   Aziza   George   Hani

Karim   Maha

VOCABULARY
Personality

2 Circle the correct words to complete what Aziza says about the people in her family.

> My sister likes meeting new people – she's very ¹outgoing / hard-working. Hani makes us all laugh – he's really ²adventurous / funny – but George is very serious and ³funny / hard-working, like my dad. My mum is really good at thinking of new ideas – she's a very ⁴creative / outgoing person. And me? Well, I always like to do new and different things, so I'm quite ⁵adventurous / funny. And we're all very intelligent, of course!

Over to you

Write a description of yourself. Write three sentences.

GRAMMAR

have got

3 Complete the description of Aziza using the words in the box.

brown   hair   jacket   pale   ~~tall~~   wearing

Aziza is ¹____tall____ and she's got ²_____ skin.
She's got black ³_____ and ⁴_____ eyes.
She's ⁵_____ trousers. She's not wearing a ⁶_____ .

4 Complete the sentences using the words in the box.

've got   Has   ~~'s got~~   haven't got   hasn't got   Have you got

1 My mum *'s got* _____ dark hair and brown eyes.
2 I _____ a brother and two sisters.
3 What time is it? _____ a watch?
4 We _____ a car; we use our bikes or public transport.
5 My brother's got a moustache, but he _____ a beard.
6 "_____ your house got a garden?" "No, but there's a big balcony."

5 Complete this paragraph with the correct form of *have got*.

From the early 1900s, most schools in Britain had a uniform to give a sense of school identity. In this picture, the three children are wearing a typical British school uniform from the 1950s. The boy ¹ *'s got* _____ short trousers and long socks. He ²_____ very short hair and a cap on his head. The older girl's uniform is very similar, but she ³_____ trousers – she's wearing a skirt. She ⁴_____ any jewellery. Both of them are wearing shirts and ties, and the school jacket, called a blazer. In many countries around the world, schools ⁵_____ still _____ some kind of uniform for their students today.

VOCABULARY
Relationships

6 Use the verbs in the box to complete the relationship expressions in bold.

are	get	get	know	like	~~see~~	spend	talk

1 We don't _____see_____ **each other** very often. 〔NC〕
2 We _____ **on** well. 〔 〕
3 We can _____ **about** everything together. 〔 〕
4 We don't _____ **in touch** very often. 〔 〕
5 We _____ **the same things**. 〔 〕
6 We _____ a lot of **time** together. 〔 〕
7 We don't _____ **each other** very well. 〔 〕
8 We _____ very **close**. 〔 〕

Over to you
Think of a person you know. Write three sentences about your relationship.

7 Which sentences in Exercise 6 describe a close relationship? Write C (close) or NC (not close) in each box.

Time**Out**

8 Find 15 more words for relatives in the word snake.

1	_aunt_	5	_____	9	_____	13	_____
2	_____	6	_____	10	_____	14	_____
3	_____	7	_____	11	_____	15	_____
4	_____	8	_____	12	_____	16	_____

EXPLORE Reading

9 **Read the first paragraph of the article. Are the sentences true or false?**

1 Nick is a journalist.   TRUE / FALSE
2 He likes formal clothes.   TRUE / FALSE
3 He likes old clothes.   TRUE / FALSE

10 **Read what Nick says about his favourite clothes. Match the clothes (1–5) with the places he got them (a–e).**

1 scarf
2 T-shirt
3 jeans
4 jacket
5 trainers

a in a shop in Australia
b in a shop in Sweden
c from a friend he worked with
d from a friend he lived with
e from his girlfriend's father

Over to you

What's your favourite outfit? Write a description and say where you got the clothes.

11 **Read the article again and try to guess the correct options.**

1 Katharine Hamnett is a journalist / designer.
2 Glastonbury is a classical / rock and folk music festival.
3 Bondi Beach is famous for surfing / sailing.
4 Stockholm at Christmas is hot / cold.

MY FAVOURITE OUTFIT

Nick Decosemo, 34, musician

Nick was a journalist, but now he has a band and is a DJ. His look is very relaxed. "All my clothes have a story. They are all second-hand." Nick likes the style of Bryan Ferry from Roxy Music and the young Mick Jagger.

JACKET
"When I worked as a journalist at a fashion magazine, my friend Gary, who's a designer, gave me this. It's by Katharine Hamnett, and it's lovely and light."

SCARF
"This belonged to my girlfriend's dad. He was a hippy in the 60s and he wore this to the first Glastonbury music festival in 1970."

T-SHIRT
"I bought this in a surf shop on Bondi Beach, in Sydney. I went to do a concert and I bought some new clothes there."

JEANS
"Last Christmas, I went to Stockholm to do a concert. It was a lovely weekend of hot wine and ice-skating – and I bought these jeans, too."

TRAINERS
"I moved house about three months ago and I found these in the flat. I think they belonged to my old flatmate, Gareth – sorry, Gareth."

1 Before you watch, write down how many people there are in your family.

2 Watch Hitin, Nilgun and Leo talking about their families. Which family is most similar to yours?

3 Watch again. Match the speakers with the family trees.

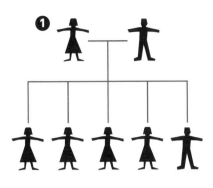  

Hitin

Nilgun

Leo

4 Watch again and circle the correct answers.
1 Hitin is the oldest / youngest child in his family.
2 His sisters give him / Hitin gives his sisters lots of presents.
3 Nilgun and her twin look / don't look the same.
4 She knows / doesn't know when her twin sister is ill.
5 Leo sees his parents every year / two years.
6 He uses the phone / Internet to talk to his parents.

5 Can you remember what Hitin, Nilgun and Leo say about their families? Complete the sentences using the words in the box. Watch again to help you.

call   close   in touch   love   lovely   make sure   mum and dad   visit   young

Hitin
1 I have a _____lovely_____ family.
2 They _____ me so much.

Nilgun
3 I'm very _____ to my twin sister.
4 We were very naughty when we were _____.
5 I usually _____ her to _____ she's OK.

Leo
6 It is very difficult for me to _____ them.
7 I feel I need to keep _____ with them.
8 It is good for me and also good for my _____.

6 Describe the people in your family. Try to use some expressions from Exercise 5.

GLOSSARY

annual /ˈænjʊəl/ (adjective): every year, or once every year
get told off (verb): If you **get told off**, someone speaks to you in an angry way because you have done something wrong.
gifts (plural noun): A **gift** is a something that you give someone; a present.
identical (adjective): **Identical twins** are formed from the same egg and are exactly the same.
naughty /ˈnɔːtiː/ (adjective): If a child is **naughty**, he/she does bad things.
youngest (adjective): The last child in a family. The first child is the **oldest**.

Getting around

9

VOCABULARY
Using transport

1 We asked these people how they get to work. Complete the answers using the phrases in the box.

> I get a taxi   I cycle   I drive   I get the bus   ~~I get the train~~   I ride a motorbike

I get the train .
The station is only five minutes from my house.

_____ .
It saves money and it helps keep me fit!

I can't drive, but I don't really like public transport, so _____ .
It's quite expensive, though.

There's a free car park at work, so _____ .

_____ .
It's faster than a car and it's easier to park.

I usually walk, but when it's raining, _____ .
It stops just outside my office.

Over to you

How often do you do these things? Write a sentence for each one.
get the bus, cycle, get a taxi, get the underground, get the train

VOCABULARY
Getting information

2 Gérard is at the Tourist Information Office. Complete his questions using the words in the box.

> best way   do you know   ~~far~~   near here   take

1 Is it _____*far*_____ ?
2 And _____ what time it opens?
3 What's the _____ to get there?
4 Is there a post office _____ ?
5 How long does it _____ to walk?

3 Complete the conversation with the questions from Exercise 2.

GÉRARD Excuse me, [1] *is there a post office near here?*

ASSISTANT Yes, it's in the square. Opposite the bank.

GÉRARD OK, thanks. [2] _____

ASSISTANT You can walk or you can get a bus.

GÉRARD [3] _____

ASSISTANT About a kilometre, more or less.

GÉRARD [4] _____

ASSISTANT Not long. About 15 minutes.

GÉRARD Great. [5] _____

ASSISTANT Nine thirty.

GRAMMAR
Comparatives and superlatives

4 Complete the sentences with the correct form of the adjectives in brackets.

1 What's __the best__ way to travel in your country? (good)
2 The metro is _____ than the bus in the mornings. (busy)
3 Riding a motorbike is _____ than flying. (dangerous)
4 The underground is _____ way to get around in London. (quick)
5 I think going by train is _____ than going by car. (interesting)
6 What's _____ way to get to the airport? (easy)

5 Think of two towns or cities you know well. Write five more comparative sentences about them. Use some of the adjectives in the box.

beautiful   busy   clean   expensive   interesting

1 *I think (San Francisco) is more beautiful than (New York).*
2 _____
3 _____
4 _____
5 _____
6 _____

VOCABULARY
Buying a ticket

6 Complete the train ticket using the words in the box.

Departure
Direct
From
Price
~~return~~

Class	Ticket type			Adult	Child	
STD	Open 1 _return_			ONE	NIL	RTH
	2 _____ date		Depart	Arrive		
	06-Oct		16.04	18.01		
3 _____		Route			5 _____	
Bournemouth		4 _____			£31.00	
To		Coach	Seat			
London Waterloo		F	71A			

7 Write the customer's questions in the correct order.

CUSTOMER Excuse me, get / how / it / London / take / long / to / to / does / ?
1 _____

ASSISTANT About two hours.

CUSTOMER And open / does / how / an / please / return / cost, / much / ?
2 _____

ASSISTANT It's £31.00.

CUSTOMER OK, and is / direct / it / ?
3 _____

ASSISTANT Yes, you don't need to change.

CUSTOMER What / leave / does / the / train / time / next / ?
4 _____

ASSISTANT At 16.04. In about half an hour.

MYEnglish

8 Read the text. Are the sentences true or false?

"I work for an American bank in Tokyo, so I speak English every day. I studied English for eight years at school and college, and I use it every day, so my English is OK – but I still find some things difficult. English pronunciation is difficult for me – and for lots of Japanese people. The sound 'th' is hard – we don't have this sound in Japanese. And I find it hard to say 'l' and 'r', too. I think people at the bank understand me, though. When I started learning English, I made mistakes with nouns, adjectives and adverbs – often it's the same word in Japanese – so I'd say 'Tokyo is a very safety city' instead of 'Tokyo is a very safe city'. I don't often make that kind of mistake now, though.

One more thing – English is everywhere in Japan! I read advertisements and everything I see in English. It helps me remember words."

Yuko, Japan

1	Yuko is a college student.	TRUE / FALSE
2	English pronunciation is difficult for Yuko.	TRUE / FALSE
3	Yuko sees lots of English in Japan.	TRUE / FALSE

Your English

9 Yuko finds some sounds difficult to pronounce in English. Here are some problem words for her.
What are the problem sounds in English for you? Add your own sounds and words to the list.

/r/	right, read
/l/	light, lead

10 Sometimes adjectives, nouns and adverbs in English are the same word in other languages. Circle the correct word in each sentence.

1 My grandfather is a very happy / happiness person.
2 You're walking very slow / slowly. Come on, hurry up!
3 Riding a motorbike is quite danger / dangerous.
4 The metro is very busy / business in the morning.
5 Taxis are quite expensive / expense.

11 Yuko says that she sees lots of things in English in Japan.
Do you see advertisements and other things in English where you live? Make a list.

EXPLORE**Writing**

12 Look at the 'On foot' section of the party invitation. Circle the correct answers and write them in the gaps.

1   a Out of   b From   c Across
2   a out of   b down   c up
3   a to   b from   c across
4   a down   b into   c from
5   a through   b down   c up
6   a out of   b up   c into

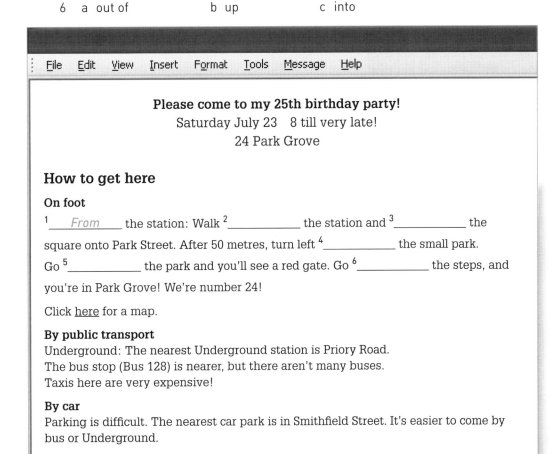

File   Edit   View   Insert   Format   Tools   Message   Help

Please come to my 25th birthday party!
Saturday July 23   8 till very late!
24 Park Grove

How to get here

On foot

¹ _From_ the station: Walk ²_____ the station and ³_____ the square onto Park Street. After 50 metres, turn left ⁴_____ the small park. Go ⁵_____ the park and you'll see a red gate. Go ⁶_____ the steps, and you're in Park Grove! We're number 24!

Click here for a map.

By public transport
Underground: The nearest Underground station is Priory Road.
The bus stop (Bus 128) is nearer, but there aren't many buses.
Taxis here are very expensive!

By car
Parking is difficult. The nearest car park is in Smithfield Street. It's easier to come by bus or Underground.

13 Read the invitation again. Which map is correct?

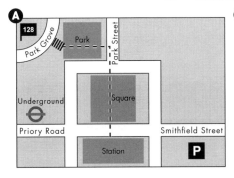
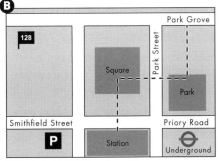
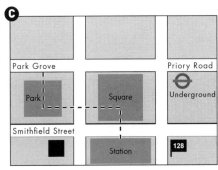

14 Look at the 'By public transport' and 'By car' sections and find:

1 two comparatives
2 two superlatives

15 Imagine you are planning a party at your home. Write notes for your invitation telling people how to get there – on foot and by public transport. Try to use at least one superlative and one comparative.

1 You are going to watch Claire talking about a long trip to Australia. Before you watch, look at this list. Which of these things do you think she talks about?

learning English ☑   snakes ☐
dolphins ☐   spiders ☐
kangaroos ☐   Sydney ☐
pizza ☐   trucks ☐

2 Watch parts 1 and 2 of the video. Tick (✓) the things from Exercise 1 that Claire mentions.

3 Watch part 1 of the video again (00:10–01:15) and circle the correct answers.

Claire Bauden was ¹18 / 19 and was a student at university in ²Australia / France. She decided to go to Perth and she stayed there for two ³years / months. At first, she ⁴could understand everything / couldn't understand anything. After six ⁵weeks / months, she felt more comfortable, so she decided to travel around Australia with a friend.

4 Watch part 2 of the video again (01:18–02:45). Claire says they decided to 'hitchhike'. Which picture shows how Claire travelled round Australia?

❶    ❷    ❸

5 Watch part 2 again. Put the pictures in the right order.

6 Claire uses some Australian words. What do you think they mean? Match the words (1–3) with the definitions (a–c).

1 g'day   a a large, empty area of land
2 the bush   b a lorry driver
3 a truckie   c hello

7 Claire and her friend hitchhiked across Australia. Would you ever hitchhike like this? Explain why / why not.

GLOSSARY

accent (noun): Your **accent** is the way you pronounce words. Some people have strong accents that are difficult to understand.
bilingual (adjective): If you are **bilingual**, you can speak two languages fluently.
hitchhike (verb): to travel by getting free rides in other people's cars and lorries
trailer (noun): something pulled behind a car or lorry
satellite phone (noun): a mobile phone that works in remote areas, for example in the desert

Getting together

VOCABULARY

Talking about films 1

1 (Circle) the correct words or phrases to complete the descriptions.

1 an animated film: a film with <u>human actors</u> / (cartoons or models)
2 a comedy: a <u>funny</u> / <u>sad</u> film that makes you <u>laugh</u> / <u>cry</u>
3 a horror film: a <u>funny</u> / <u>scary</u> film about <u>nice</u> / <u>horrible</u> things
4 a drama: a <u>funny</u> / <u>serious</u> film with an interesting story
5 a romantic film: a film about <u>love</u> / <u>war</u>
6 an action film: <u>a boring</u> / <u>an exciting</u> film where <u>a lot</u> / <u>not a lot</u> of things happen
7 a documentary: a film about <u>real</u> / <u>imaginary</u> people or things
8 a science-fiction film: a film set in the <u>past</u> / <u>future</u> or another part of the universe

VOCABULARY

Suggestions

2 Write the words in the correct order to complete the conversation.

> **ANNA** If you're not doing anything this evening, ¹ <u>you / come / like / would / to</u>
> _would you like to come_ over to my house? ² <u>could / We / get</u>
> _____ a pizza and watch a film.
>
> **SONIA** ³ <u>good / sounds / That</u> _____ .
>
> **ANNA** OK. I've got an old Hitchcock film we could watch.
>
> **SONIA** Hmm. ⁴ <u>not / I'm / sure</u> _____ . I don't usually like thrillers.
> ⁵ <u>we / DVD / Why / rent / don't / a</u> _____ ?
>
> **ANNA** ⁶ <u>with / me / Fine</u> _____ .

GRAMMAR

Present progressive for future arrangements

3 Complete the sentences using the verbs in the box in the present progressive.

| arrive   come   come back   fly   go   ~~stay~~   wait   not work |

1 Dr Sharma's here for a conference. He _'s staying_ in a hotel in the centre of town. [N]
2 They _____ to my house this evening to watch a film. ☐
3 I _____ to Qatar tomorrow on the midday flight. ☐
4 We _____ camping in Greece this summer. ☐
5 The train _____ at the station. ☐
6 I _____ from my trip on Sunday night. ☐
7 Where are you? We _____ for you! ☐
8 She's got baby twins, so she _____ at the moment. ☐

4 Which sentences in Exercise 3 are about now and which are about future arrangements? Write N (now) or F (future) in the boxes.

5 Complete the time expressions in bold with *in*, *on* or *at* if necessary. Some expressions don't need a preposition.

1 They're leaving __*on*__ **Saturday morning**.

2 We're going to Morocco _____ **next month**.

3 I'm going to the dentist's _____ **this afternoon**.

4 My grandfather's having his 90th birthday party _____ **14th May**!

5 We're leaving _____ **tonight**.

6 They're having another meeting _____ **tomorrow**.

7 Their train's arriving _____ **6.15**.

8 I'm going on holiday _____ **August**.

6 Look at Liz's desk. Tick (✓) the true sentences and correct the false ones.

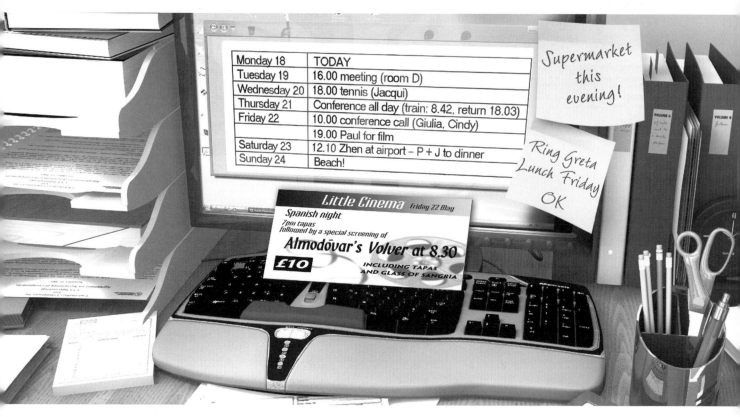

Monday 18	TODAY
Tuesday 19	16.00 meeting (room D)
Wednesday 20	18.00 tennis (Jacqui)
Thursday 21	Conference all day (train: 8.42, return 18.03)
Friday 22	10.00 conference call (Giulia, Cindy)
	19.00 Paul for film
Saturday 23	12.10 Zhen at airport – P + J to dinner
Sunday 24	Beach!

Supermarket this evening!

Little Cinema Friday 22 May
Spanish night
7pm tapas
followed by a special screening of
Almodóvar's Volver at 8.30
£10
INCLUDING TAPAS
AND GLASS OF SANGRIA

Ring Greta Lunch Friday OK

Liz, Scotland

Over to you

Look at your diary and write three sentences about your arrangements.

1 She's playing tennis on Wednesday morning.
   She's playing tennis on Wednesday evening / at 6 pm on Wednesday.

2 She's going shopping this evening.
   _____

3 She's not working in the office on Thursday.
   _____

4 She's speaking to Giulia on Friday afternoon.
   _____

5 She's seeing friends on Saturday evening.
   _____

6 She's having a meeting tomorrow afternoon.
   _____

7 She's staying at home on Friday evening.
   _____

8 She's meeting Zhen at the airport on Sunday.
   _____

VOCABULARY

Talking about
films 2

7 Complete the film review using the words and phrases in the box.

character   directed by   ~~drama~~   funny   it's about   set in   stars

http://www.dvdrelease.co.uk

Volver

Volver (2006) is a ¹____drama____ written and ²_____ Pedro Almodóvar. It is
³_____ a village in Spain, and ⁴_____ a family – two sisters, their aunt and the
teenage daughter of one of the sisters. Another ⁵_____ is the sisters' dead mother,
who comes back to help them in a difficult time; *volver* means 'to return' in Spanish.
It ⁶_____ Penélope Cruz, but the cast really work as a team; in fact, six actresses
shared the Best Actress award at the Cannes Film Festival. *Volver* is a warm, ⁷_____
film about the relationship between women.

☆☆☆☆☆

TimeOut

8 How much do you know about the cinema? Do the quiz!

1 Who directed the film *2001 A Space Odyssey*?
 a Ridley Scott   **b** George Lucas   **c** Stanley Kubrick

2 What nationality is the actor Gael García Bernal?
 a Mexican   **b** Argentinian   **c** Spanish

3 Where does the director Ang Lee come from?
 a The United States   **b** Taiwan   **c** Korea

4 Which city is the Bollywood film industry based in?
 a Delhi   **b** Kolkata   **c** Mumbai

5 Which rock band made the film *Tommy*?
 a Pink Floyd   **b** The Who   **c** Rolling Stones

6 Which country makes the most films in Arabic?
 a Egypt   **b** Tunisia   **c** Syria

7 Which film is NOT Chinese?
 a *Red Sorghum*   **b** *Farewell My Concubine*   **c** *Spirited Away*

8 Who is the voice of Donkey in the *Shrek* films?
 a Mike Myers   **b** Antonio Banderas   **c** Eddie Murphy

Answers
1c 2a 3b 4c ('The old name of the city was Bombay.)
5b 6a 7c (It's Japanese.) 8c

EXPLORE**Reading**

9 Look at the page from the *Summer in the City* programme. Tick (✓) the kinds of events that are featured.

Theatre	✓	Jazz	☐
Classical music	☐	Folk music	☐
Film	☐	Walks	☐
Dance	☐	Rock music	☐
Children's events	☐	Talks	☐

10 Are these sentences true or false?

1 All the music events are free. TRUE / FALSE
2 You don't have to pay to see the film. TRUE / FALSE
3 The most expensive event is a live show. TRUE / FALSE
4 Adults cannot sleep in the park after *Clowns*. TRUE / FALSE

11 Which event do you choose if ...

1 you want to dance until late at night?
2 you are interested in history?
3 you want to take your eight-year-old daughter out?
4 you want to have a drink and listen to some relaxing music?

Summer in the City

Saturday 12 July

CINEMA UNDER THE STARS
Piazza Grande 22.00

The Man Without a Past
by Aki Kaurismaki (Finland, 2003)

Free

SPECIAL EVENT
Arena Sport 21.30

Fura dels Baus
Spectacular performance by the celebrated Catalan theatre company in their new all-women production, *Imperium*

€30
Information and tickets from Tourist Information Office, Piazza Grande
Mon–Sat 14.00–19.00

KIDS' SUMMER
Guasto Gardens 20.00

Clowns

A fun show for the under-12s, inspired by Fellini's clowns. After the show, kids and their families are invited to sleep under the stars in the park!

Free, but book in advance
339 3450228

SCANDELLARA FESTIVAL
Scandellara Park 21.00–02.00

Jurassic Rock in concert 22.00
Plus DJ

Free

CITY WALKS
Starting from Piazza Piccola 21.00

Secrets of the Middle Ages: the city in the 13th and 14th century
The walk lasts approximately two hours.

€8 Book in advance 348 4499321

OPEN-AIR JAZZ
Via del Porto 21.30

Music from the Max Aurora trio

Entrance and first drink €5

CLASSICAL COURTYARD
De Pisis Gallery main courtyard 21.30

Music by Schubert, Beethoven and Dvorak
Donatella Virzi, piano

Free

1 Before you watch, look at this list of types of film and tick (✓) the ones you like.

		Exercise 1	Exercise 2
1	comedies	☐	*A*
2	Indian cinema	☐	☐
3	romantic comedies	☐	☐
4	serious documentaries	☐	☐
5	romantic love stories	☐	☐

2 Watch Amanda and Hitin talking about films. Who talks about the types of films in Exercise 1? Write A (Amanda) or H (Hitin).

Amanda

Hitin

3 Watch Amanda again (00:10–00:39) and (circle) the correct answers.

1 Why can Amanda go to the cinema without paying?
   a) She works there.   b) Her husband works there.
2 Why did they go to see films more often in the past?
   a) Because now they need a babysitter for their son.
   b) Because their son doesn't like films.
3 What kind of films do Amanda and her husband go to see?
   a) science-fiction films   b) comedies and more serious films

4 Complete the information about Indian films using the words in the box. Watch Hitin again (00:40–01:54) to help you.

~~characters~~ family friends fun happy love story songs

Indian films have 'larger than life' [1] _characters_ , and they are really [2]_____ .

They are usually a romantic [3]_____ , and most films have a [4]_____

ending. They are different from American movies because they have a lot of

[5]_____ . Indian films reflect Indian culture and are usually about

[6]_____ and [7]_____ .

5 Match the beginnings and endings of the sentences to make sentences that Amanda and Hitin say. Watch again to check.

1	I like ...	a	when I was a small baby.
2	We also see ...	b	Indian cinema.
3	I'm a huge fan of ...	c	some serious documentaries.
4	My love for Indian cinema began ...	d	romantic comedy.

6 Describe the type of films people in your country like.

GLOSSARY

bonding (noun): a close feeling or relationship between people
ending (noun): the end; the way a story or film finishes
for free (expression): If you can do something **for free**, you don't pay any money.
larger than life (adjective phrase): A person who is **larger than life** seems very interesting or different from normal people.
look after (verb): If you **look after** children, you care for them and keep them safe.
projectionist (noun): A **projectionist** is the person who operates the equipment (the **projector**) to show the film in a cinema.

Journeys

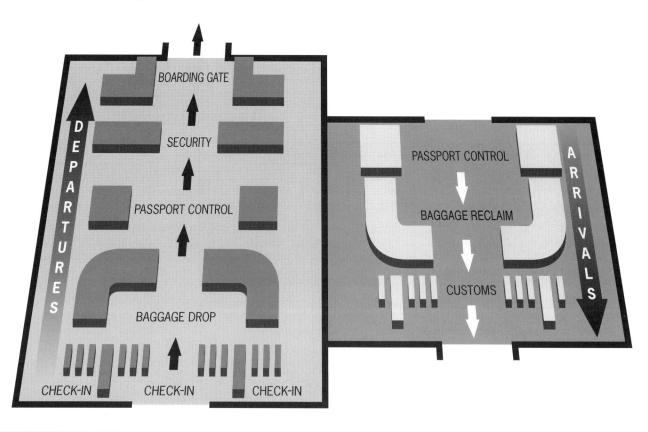

1 Find places in the airport where you do these things.

When you start your journey, ...

1 you and your bags are checked here for dangerous things.   _security_

2 you go here to show your ticket or boarding pass before you fly.   _____

3 your plane leaves from here.   _____

4 you leave your big bags here.   _____

When you arrive at your destination, ...

5 your bags arrive here.   _____

6 you have to go through here before you leave the airport.   _____

7 you show your passport here.   _____

2 Complete the airport sentences using the words in the box.

anything	bag	belt	gate	keys	laptop	~~luggage~~	pack	passport

1 Do you have any hand _luggage_ ?   ☐ C

2 Are you wearing a _____ ?   ☐

3 Can I see your _____ and ticket, please?   ☐

4 Did you _____ your bag yourself?   ☐

5 Do you have a _____ in your bag?   ☐

6 Boarding is at 10.25 from _____ 12.   ☐

7 Do you have any _____ in your bag?   ☐

8 Would you open your _____ , please?   ☐

9 Are you carrying _____ for anyone else?   ☐

3 Where do you hear the sentences in Exercise 2? Write C (check-in) or S (security).

GRAMMAR

Articles

Montse, Spain

4 Number the sentences 1–5 to tell Montse's story.

a ☐ At the end of my holiday, I bought a special bag and put the cat in it.

b ☐ I took it to my holiday apartment and gave it food every day.

c ☐ In the end, I paid a lot of money to bring the cat into the country; I think I have the most expensive cat in the world!

d ☐1☐ I love cats, and when I was on holiday in Greece, I found a beautiful little cat.

e ☐ I had no problems when I left Greece, but when I arrived at the airport in my country, the Customs officials took the cat from me.

5 Match the phrases from the story (1–10) with the rules (a–f).

1   at **the** end of my holiday
2   I bought **a** special bag
3   put **the** cat in it
4   gave it food
5   **the** most expensive cat
6   in **the** world
7   I love cats
8   **a** beautiful little cat
9   at **the** airport
10 took **the** cat from me

a   Use *a/an* to talk about a person or thing for the first time. ☐2☐☐

b   Use *the* when the reader or listener knows which thing. ☐☐

c   Use – (no article) to talk about things in general. ☐☐

d   Use *the* with some time expressions. ☐

e   Use *the* with some place expressions. ☐☐

f   Use *the* with some adjectives. ☐

VOCABULARY

Storytelling expressions

Elke, Germany

6 Complete Elke's travel story using the expressions in the box.

> ~~a few years ago~~   and then   at the time   I was with   In the end
> in the middle of   It was quite frightening   the south of

Well, this was ¹ *a few years ago* in Africa. I was in Tanzania
² _____ . I was in the Selous Park in ³ _____ the
country, on a safari trip. ⁴ _____ my husband, the driver of
the car and another guide. We crossed a dry river, ⁵ _____
the driver stopped the car because there was a huge mother elephant
⁶ _____ the road, about ten metres in front of us. She was
dangerous because her baby was near; we couldn't go back and we
couldn't continue driving. ⁷ _____ , the elephant walked
away to her baby. ⁸ _____ , but I got some great photos!

VOCABULARY

Talking about
a journey

Over to you

Talk about a
journey you went
on. Use some
expressions from
Exercise 7.

7 Cross out the words or expressions that are *not* correct.

1 We booked / went / found seats on a flight to New York.
2 We drove / went / waited to the airport.
3 We showed our passport / shopping / ticket at check-in.
4 The flight was on time / delayed / checked.
5 We cancelled / caught / missed our connection in Amsterdam.
6 We spent / waited / wanted six hours in the airport.
7 The airport was very comfortable / uncomfortable / delayed.
8 The flight left / started / took off at 11.30 at night.
9 The plane checked / landed / arrived in New York the next afternoon.
10 We stayed / were / delayed in a three-star hotel on Broadway.

MYEnglish

8 Read what Nadya says, and choose the correct way to
complete the sentences.

1 Nadya speaks good / a little English.
2 She likes reading / listening to English.

" I really like travelling, and now I can speak a little bit of English, I see and hear
it everywhere, even in my own country. I like to practise reading signs and
advertisements, because my language uses a different alphabet, but when
people speak to me, I get very nervous and I don't always understand. I try to
imagine the questions that people can ask me and I practise conversations with
myself. And sometimes I ask people for information just to practise! I smile and
ask politely, so I think it's OK. "

Nadya, Ukraine

9 Which communication strategies does Nadya use?

1 She reads words on signs. ☑
2 She practises pronouncing words she sees. ☐
3 She learns and practises key words before she travels. ☐
4 She imagines the questions people will ask. ☐
5 She practises conversations with herself. ☐
6 She practises expressions to check she understands. ☐
7 She practises expressions to ask people to repeat. ☐
8 She tries asking people questions. ☐

Your English

10 Tick (✓) the strategies you use. Write ! for strategies you would
like to try.

11 Do you remember these questions you can use to ask people for
help when you don't understand?
Complete them using the words in the box.

| how much | ~~say~~ | slow down | spell | understand | which |

1 Sorry, could you _____say_____ that again, please?
2 I'm sorry, I don't _____.
3 Could you _____ the name for me, please?
4 Sorry, _____ did you say? €3.50?
5 Sorry, can you _____ a bit?
6 Sorry, _____ platform?

EXPLORE Writing

12 Read the letter and ⟨circle⟩ the correct words.

1 Ms Bruckner travelled by plane /⟨ferry⟩.
2 She is writing to the travel company / a friend.
3 She went to Italy / Greece.
4 The boat was delayed / cancelled.
5 She wants to book another journey / an apology and some money.

24 September

Dear Sir or Madam

1 I am writing <u>to complain</u> about a journey with your company on 4 August from Brindisi, Italy, to Patras, Greece.

2 Our ferry <u>was delayed</u> by ten hours, but your <u>staff</u> didn't give us any information, and there was no shop or café to buy any food or drinks. When we got on the boat, it was dirty and uncomfortable. There were no <u>free seats</u>, and my three children and I slept on the floor in the bar.

3 I am not <u>satisfied</u> with your service and I hope <u>to receive</u> an apology and <u>some compensation</u> for our uncomfortable journey. I look forward to your reply.

Yours faithfully

Clara Bruckner

Clara Bruckner

13 How is the letter organised? Which paragraph (1, 2 or 3) ...

a asks for a reply? ☐
b says why Clara is writing? ☐
c gives information about the problem? ☐

14 Match the <u>underlined</u> words and expressions in the letter with the definitions.

1 the people who work for a company *staff* _____
2 places to sit _____
3 to say I am not happy _____
4 to get _____
5 was late _____
6 happy _____
7 some money _____

15 Find expressions in the letter that are used to ...

1 start the letter _____
2 say why you are writing _____
3 say you want the person to write back to you _____
4 end the letter _____

flight 15 hours delayed
no information
no food, expensive drinks
no seats in airport, sat on floor
old, dirty plane

16 You had a very bad flight with BestOne airlines. Use the notes on the left to write a letter to complain.

1 Before you watch, look at these countries. Which ones, if any, have you visited?

Croatia Italy Japan Mexico Poland the USA

2 Watch Justyna and Luis talking about trips. Which two countries did they visit?

Justyna

Luis

3 Watch again and (circle) the correct answers.

Justyna
1 Justyna went to Croatia on holiday / (for work).
2 Justyna thought Croat and Polish were similar / very different.
3 'False friends' are words that sound the same but have a different meaning / spelling.
4 Justyna wanted to ask how long it would take to iron a shirt / some trousers.
5 *Godzina* means 'hour' in Polish and 'week' / 'year' in Croat.

Luis
6 Luis flew over the Grand Canyon in a helicopter / plane.
7 He sat in the back / front seat.
8 The floor was made of metal / glass.
9 They flew for an hour / a couple of hours.

4 Complete the sentences using the adjectives in the box. Watch again to check.

| amazing confident excited offended |

1 I went to a conference in Croatia, and I was very _____ – I was quite _____ .
2 I wanted to ask the lady how long it would take to iron my trousers, and she got quite _____ .
3 It was an _____ experience that I will never forget.

flying over the Grand Canyon

5 Justyna talks about 'false friends' – words that sound similar to a word in your language but have a different meaning. What 'false friends' can you think of?

6 Describe a trip you have taken. Where did you go? What did you do? What did you like / not like?

GLOSSARY

conference (noun): a big meeting with talks on a particular subject
canyon (noun): a big valley with steep sides, like the Grand Canyon in Arizona, USA
cliff (noun): a high wall of rock, often (but not always) near the sea
iron (verb): to make clothes flat and smooth
offended (adjective): If you are **offended**, your feelings are hurt.

Are you OK?

VOCABULARY

The body and health

1 Complete the names of the parts of the body.

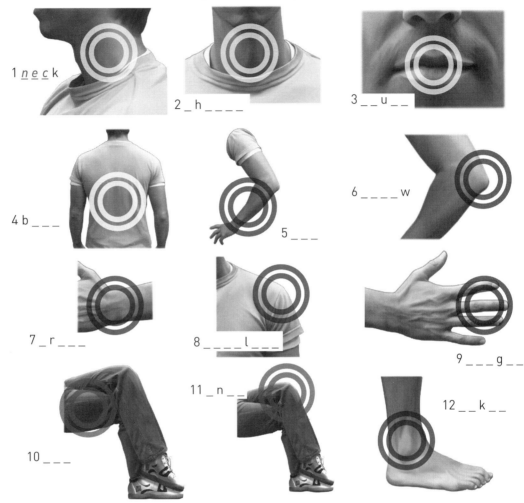

1 <u>n e c</u> k

2 _ h _ _ _ _

3 _ _ u _ _

4 b _ _ _

5 _ _ _

6 _ _ _ _ w

7 _ r _ _ _

8 _ _ _ _ l _ _ _

9 _ _ _ g _ _

10 _ _ _

11 _ n _ _

12 _ _ k _ _

2 Use the words and expressions in the box to complete the medicine instructions.

allergic to   children under 12   every four to six hours   Keep away from
sore throat   ~~symptoms~~   WARNING!

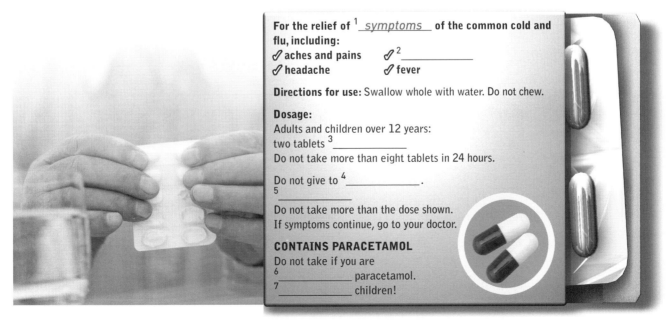

For the relief of ¹ <u>symptoms</u> of the common cold and flu, including:
- aches and pains
- ² _____
- headache
- fever

Directions for use: Swallow whole with water. Do not chew.

Dosage:
Adults and children over 12 years:
two tablets ³ _____
Do not take more than eight tablets in 24 hours.

Do not give to ⁴ _____.
⁵ _____
Do not take more than the dose shown.
If symptoms continue, go to your doctor.

CONTAINS PARACETAMOL
Do not take if you are
⁶ _____ paracetamol.
⁷ _____ children!

3 Look at Gabor and Lydia's problems. Circle the correct words in the advice below. Then mark each piece of advice G (Gabor) or L (Lydia).

I've got a headache.

I want to stay healthy at work.

Gabor

Lydia

1 Don't sit / Sit near the air-conditioner. It's bad for your eyes and skin.
L

2 You *should / shouldn't* see a doctor – it might be something serious.
☐

3 You *should / shouldn't* go out for a walk – it's not good to be inside all day.
☐

4 Get / Don't get some plants – they'll make your desk look nicer.
☐

5 You *should / shouldn't* put salt water in your ears. It can help the pain stop. But don't use really hot water!
☐

6 Take / Don't take a paracetamol and lie down for half an hour.
☐

7 You *should / shouldn't* keep the window closed – you need fresh air!
☐

8 Listen / Don't listen to loud music!
☐

4 Françoise wants to keep fit. Write three pieces of advice for her.

5 Read the advice on how to stay healthy at work. Match the beginnings (1–6) with the endings (a–f).

1 ☐ *f* You should sit near a window if ...
2 ☐ If you want to improve the appearance of your office, ...
3 ☐ You should change the colour of your office walls if ...
4 ☐ You should open a window in your office ...
5 ☐ If you want to keep fit, ...
6 ☐ If you don't want to get back pain, ...

a ... get some plants.
b ... if possible.
c ... make sure you have the right chair.
d ... you feel bored.
e ... use the stairs, not the lift.
f ... you can.

Collocations

6 Complete the diagrams using the words in the box.

a meeting   a party   a train   fun   lunch   money   tablets   ~~time~~

_____   _____

have

_____   _____

spend

time

_____

take

_____   _____

7 Complete the sentences with collocations from Exercise 6.

1 Do you want to ____have____ ____lunch____ next week? There's a new café on the high street.

2 It'll be quicker to _____ _____ – the traffic is always bad at this time of day.

3 Did you _____ _____ at Isabel's party?

4 We should _____ _____ in the office next week. We need to discuss this face to face.

5 I know I should _____ more _____ with my family, but I'm too busy at work!

TimeOut

8 Find 15 more parts of the body.

L	Q	Z	E	W	Y	W	T	U	S	P	I	G	S	M
Y	K	Y	U	B	F	U	H	R	S	N	A	D	Q	D
E	T	I	V	O	Z	T	R	U	M	K	Z	L	T	Q
N	E	C	K	H	N	O	O	Z	F	C	I	R	L	N
C	S	V	I	E	Q	E	A	E	U	T	L	N	J	U
C	T	M	Y	A	B	G	T	K	U	S	A	B	K	T
T	O	U	G	D	Y	Z	Y	Z	N	E	E	A	O	F
F	M	S	P	O	V	P	Q	N	I	E	W	C	D	A
D	A	C	B	U	O	K	S	X	M	S	E	K	K	C
T	C	L	H	E	S	Y	R	F	I	N	G	E	R	E
G	H	E	E	A	N	K	L	E	W	J	R	A	P	F
F	U	F	H	J	L	S	M	V	X	H	E	Z	S	N
G	L	B	N	M	U	F	O	O	T	V	Y	K	V	X
Y	J	E	M	O	U	T	H	I	L	M	L	C	L	O
I	Q	M	G	P	C	H	S	H	O	U	L	D	E	R

EXPLOREReading

9 Read the advice about flying. Put these headings (1–3) in the correct places (A–C).

1 Before you fly
2 Flying with children
3 In the plane

✈ STAY HEALTHY WHEN YOU FLY

A _____

1 Take lots of water to the airport with you. Drink it regularly.
2 Make sure you have lots of time to get to the airport. Check that the roads are clear or the trains are on time.
3 Before you get on your flight, go for a quick walk in the airport to get some exercise.
4 _____

B _____

5 Don't drink coffee or alcohol.
6 Get up and have a walk for five or ten minutes every hour. Don't just sit in your seat.
7 Keep any medicine you need in your hand luggage.
8 _____

C _____

9 Call the airline before you travel. Ask if they do anything special for children.
10 Give yourself lots and lots of time to do anything! Children don't always move quickly.
11 Bring something for children to do in the airport and on the plane.
12 _____

---

10 Write the three extra pieces of advice in the correct sections of the leaflet.

a Read a book or do a puzzle before you get on the flight. It will help you stop feeling nervous.
b Bring some snacks – children might not like the food on the plane.
c Don't sit with your legs crossed. Move your legs to get some exercise in your seat.

11 Match the pictures (a–f) with the correct piece of advice in the leaflet.

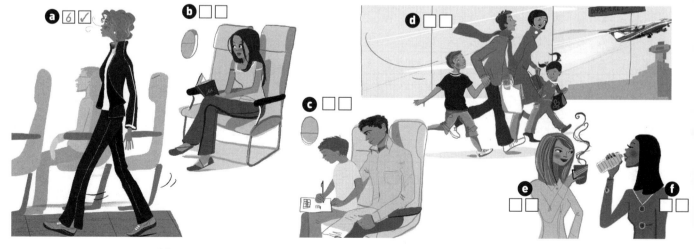

12 Look at the pictures in Exercise 11 and decide if they are things you *should* or *shouldn't* do according to the leaflet. Put a tick (✓) beside the things you *should* do and put a cross (✗) beside the things you *shouldn't* do.

1 Before you watch, look at the photos. Which do you think is most important for a healthy lifestyle?

exercise ☐

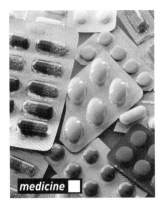
medicine ☐

sleep ☐

diet ☐

2 Watch Lona talking about a healthy lifestyle. Number the photos in Exercise 1 in the order she talks about them.

3 Watch again and (circle) the correct answers.

1 Lona likes to sleep (eight) / ten hours a day.
2 She thinks going to the gym is boring / fun.
3 She goes to dance classes once / a couple of times a week.
4 She prefers to eat white / brown rice and wholemeal / white bread.
5 She buys organic food / goes to a restaurant when she has some money.
6 Her family uses Ayurvedic / Western medicine at home.

4 Match the phrases to make sentences. Watch again to check.

1	She sleeps	a	honey	i	because it gives energy.
2	She drinks	b	for eight hours	ii	when she isn't feeling well.
3	She takes	c	turmeric in warm milk	iii	to feel good.

5 Match the beginnings and endings of the sentences. Watch again to check.

1 It's really important to ...
2 Another thing that's really important is ...
3 I hate activities like ...
4 I tend to eat ...
5 There are some other things that ...

a ... exercise.
b ... I like to take.
c ... respect one's pattern of sleeping.
d ... going to the gym.
e ... things like brown rice.

6 Describe your lifestyle. Is it like Lona's? Try to use expressions from Exercise 5.

GLOSSARY

Ayurvedic medicine (noun): traditional Indian medicine
components (plural noun): the different parts of something
side effect (noun): A **side effect** of a medicine is an extra, negative effect.
turmeric (noun): a yellow spice
wholemeal (adjective): **Wholemeal** bread is made from brown flour, not white, so it's more natural.

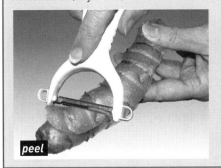
peel

grate

strain

13 Experiences

1 Match the sentence beginnings (1–12) with the correct endings (a–l). There may be more than one possible answer.

1	I've never met	a	a book in English.
2	I've never used	b	a cigarette.
3	I've never smoked	c	a telephone meeting.
4	I've never eaten	d	a member of a gym.
5	I've never been	e	watching sport on TV.
6	I've never played	f	a famous person.
7	I've never worked	g	a horror film.
8	I've never read	h	to be rich.
9	I've never liked	i	an MP3 player.
10	I've never had	j	golf.
11	I've never seen	k	after midnight.
12	I've never wanted	l	Japanese food.

2 Complete the table. Use the sentences in Exercise 1 to help you.

	Verb	Past participle
Regular verbs (–ed)	_use_	_used_
	_____	_____
	_____	_____
	_____	_____
	_____	_____
	_____	_____
Irregular	meet	_____
	eat	_____
	be	_____
	read	_____
	have	_____
	see	_____

Over to you

Write three things you've never done and three things you've always wanted to do. Use verbs from the table in Exercise 2.

3 Label the postcards using the words in the box.

castle   city walls   fountain   museum   palace
ruins   sculpture   statue   tomb   waterfall

1 _castle_   2 _____   3 _____   4 _____

5 _____   6 _____   7 _____   8 _____   9 _____   10 _____

4 Complete the postcard using the correct past participle of the verbs in the box.

eat   meet   see   want

Hi!
Well, I've always ¹_____ to come here, and it's a beautiful place! We're having a great time – we've ²_____ all the sights and ³_____ some great food. And we've ⁴_____ some really nice people, too. Wish you were here!
Kirsten

Mark Edwards
43 Laurel Lane
Ashworth
Beds
HP9 4QQ

5 Complete the article using the questions in the box.

Over to you

Write your own answers to the six questions in Exercise 5.

a   What's the nicest hotel you've ever stayed in?
b   What's the most interesting place you've seen in your own country?
c   Have you had any bad experiences while travelling?
d   ~~What's the most beautiful place you've ever been to?~~
e   What's the strangest thing you've ever eaten when you're travelling?
f   Which country have you always wanted to visit?

My holidays

Michelle Giaquinto is from Australia. At the moment, she is working as a cook in a vegetarian restaurant in Italy. She has travelled to over 30 countries, including Mexico, Thailand, Nepal, Pakistan, Morocco, Guatemala, Turkey and many countries in Africa and Europe.

1 *What's the most beautiful place you've ever been to?*

It's difficult to choose the 'most beautiful' place I've visited, as every country has its personal bests. But I have very happy memories of the giant Himalayan mountains I walked through for three weeks in Nepal.

2 _____

I stayed in a beautiful little 'riad', or guesthouse, in Marrakech, Morocco. It wasn't very big, but it had a green courtyard with a fountain in the middle. The colourful tiles everywhere gave it an exotic feel, too.

3 _____

The strangest thing I've tried were the fried crickets on the street in Bangkok, Thailand. You get three or four on a stick, and they're not bad – sweet and crunchy.

4 _____

I have always been very lucky in my travels, but someone stole my bag on a train when I was in India. Getting very ill in a lonely part of Pakistan wasn't very nice, either.

5 _____

I still haven't visited Indonesia, a country with a very interesting culture and excellent diving sites to explore.

6 _____

Australia has so many interesting places to visit, as it's so large and diverse. But my favourites are the sights along the Great Barrier Reef, North Queensland. I also love the big, open spaces of our deserts and National Parks, especially Uluru National Park.

GRAMMAR

Present perfect
(*Have you
ever ... ?*)

6 Complete the questions using the past participle of the verbs in the box. Then complete the answers with *Yes* or *No*.

be   be   eat   ~~hear~~   hear   see

1   _Have you (ever) heard_   of Machu Picchu?
    _____Yes_____ , it's in Peru, I think.

2   _____ to New York?
    _____ , it's a fantastic city.

3   _____ Thai curry?
    _____ , I haven't. I don't really like spicy food.

4   _____ the Pyramids in Cairo?
    _____ , they're incredible!

5   _____ to France?
    _____ , but I've only been to Paris. What's the rest of the country like?

6   _____ of Uluru National Park?
    _____ , I have, but I've never been there.

Over to you

Write your own
answers to the
questions in
Exercise 6.

MYEnglish

7 Read what Piet says and answer the questions.

1   Where does Piet work?
2   Why does he use English at work?
3   What two problems does he say he has with English?

Piet, Netherlands

> I work in the international department of a large bank in The Hague. I have a lot of colleagues who are not from my country, so I often use English at work. I learned English at school, of course, and when I was a student at university, I spent six months working for an international bank in Germany. That was a very good experience because the official language at work was English. I think my English is good now, but I know my pronunciation isn't perfect – I think the *th* sounds are very difficult. But I don't think this is a big problem – my colleagues understand me! One grammar mistake I often make is using the present perfect instead of the past simple, like *I have played tennis yesterday* instead of *I played tennis yesterday*. I think I need to practise more!

Your English

8 Answer these questions.

1   Who do you use English with?
    • English-speaking people (from Britain, Ireland, the USA, Australia, etc.)
    • people from other countries?
2   Where do you use English?
    • in your country?
    • in English-speaking countries?
    • in other countries?

9 Do you have difficulty pronouncing *th* sounds? Go to the DVD-ROM for some practice.

EXPLORE Writing

10 Read these two extracts from a website where tourists write reviews of places they visit. Would you like to visit either of these places? Why? / Why not?

File   Edit   View   Favorites   Tools   Help

Address | www.tripreviewer.com | Go | Links »

Find the best things to do

Museum of Archaeology and Prehistory

Rating: ◉◉◉◉○

This is one of the most interesting museums in the town. It is in the centre, on the north side of the main square.

It has impressive Roman and Egyptian collections, and objects from Africa, Asia and Peru. In the Prehistory section, there are life-size models of dinosaurs.

The museum is open every day except Monday, from 10.00 am to 6.00 pm.

Adults €4.60 Under 16 €2.

Royal Gardens

Rating: ◉◉◉◉○

This is the town's biggest open space and the best place to go for some fresh air. The number 13 bus goes past it, or you can walk from the centre in 15 minutes.

The park has a café, a children's play area and a small lake, where you can rent a boat. And there's lots of grass to sit or lie on, or play Frisbee, football or cricket.

Open from 7.00 am to 7.00 pm. In summer, the park is open late and there's live music every evening.

---

11 Which text(s) includes this information? Write M (museum) and/or P (park).

1 where it is   M ☐   4 what activities you can do there ☐ ☐
2 how to get there   ☐ ☐   5 opening days/times   ☐ ☐
3 what you can see there   ☐ ☐   6 ticket prices   ☐ ☐

12 Complete these superlative expressions from the extracts in Exercise 10.

1 This is _____ _____ _____ most interesting museums in the town.

2 This is the town's _____ open space ...

3 ... and the _____ _____ to go for some fresh air.

13 (Circle) the correct words.

1 It has / is impressive Roman and Egyptian collections.
2 There / They are life-size models.
3 The park has / is a café.
4 There is / are lots of grass.
5 There / It is live music.

14 Complete the phrases with the correct prepositions, according to the websites.

1 It is _____ the centre, ...
2 _____ the north side _____ the main square.
3 The number 13 bus goes _____ it, ...
4 ... or you can walk _____ the centre _____ 15 minutes.

15 Correct these lists of things. Use commas (,) and write *and* where necessary.

1 objects from Africa Asia Peru
2 The park has a café a children's play area a small lake.

Look at the texts again to check.

16 Think of two places/things in your town/area that would be interesting for visitors. Think about what information you want to include (look at the list in Exercise 11) and write your recommendations.

1   Before you watch, look at part of the VSO website. VSO is a charity organisation that works in developing countries. Do you know other, similar organisations? Is there a similar organisation in your country?

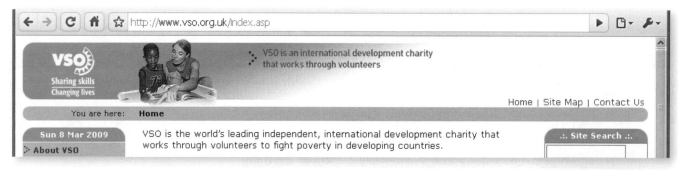

2   Watch parts 1 and 2 of the video. Choose the best summary of what Patrizia says.

Patrizia

a   Patrizia did voluntary work in Vietnam. She enjoyed the experience and now she would like to go to work in Africa.

b   Patrizia went on holiday to Vietnam. She enjoyed the experience, so she went to work in Africa as a marketing and communications officer.

3   Watch part 1 again (00:11–01:07). Tick (✓) the things in the advertisement that Patrizia mentions about her time with VSO.

Voluntary Service Overseas

- ❀ working with local colleagues ☑
- ❀ sharing professional skills ☐
- ❀ cultural experiences ☐
- ❀ learning new languages ☐
- ❀ an insight into working abroad ☐
- ❀ interesting travel ☐

4   Watch part 2 again (01:07–01:58) and circle the correct answers.

1   Patrizia would like to work in Africa / Asia.
2   She would like to use her medical / marketing and communication skills
3   She went to Ethiopia for work / a holiday.
4   She really enjoyed / didn't enjoy her time in Ethiopia.

5   Look at the different ways Patrizia talks about work. Watch again and complete the sentences.

```
1                              … the opportunity to work __alongside__ local colleagues, and this …
2                       … have an insight into working _____ a foreign country, a very …
3               … and given me the desire to work _____, and this has now …
4         … my main ambition, and that is to work _____ an international development organisation.
5            … where I would like to work is _____ a country in Africa where …
6  … marketing and communication skills, possibly to work _____ a health organisation.
7              … given me the motivation to go and work _____ Africa and maybe in a different …
```

6   Would you like to do something like VSO? Explain why / why not.

GLOSSARY

volunteer (noun): a person who does something to help people – usually without being paid
insight (noun): the ability to understand what something is like
ambition (noun): something you really want to do in the future
international development (noun): projects to help improve the quality of life in countries around the world
diversity (noun): when many different types of thing or people are included in something
motivation (noun): your need or reason for doing something

Choices

VOCABULARY

too much,
enough,
not enough

1   Read the questionnaire and (circle) the answers that are most true for you.

Is your lifestyle good for you?

1   How much coffee or tea do you drink a day?

    A none   **B** between one and three cups   **C** more than three cups

2   How much exercise do you do?

    A 30–60 minutes every day   **B** 30–60 minutes a week   **C** none

3   How many hours do you sleep?

    A 6–8 hours a night   **B** 8–11 hours a night   **C** 3–4 hours a night

4   How much water do you drink?

    A more than one litre a day   **B** less than one litre a day   **C** none

5   How many hours do you work?

    A 20–35 hours a week   **B** 35–40 hours a week   **C** 50–60 hours a week

6   How often do you eat fast food or sweets?

    A never   **B** fewer than four times a week   **C** more than four times a week

7   How often do you eat fish?

    A more than two times a week   **B** fewer than two times a week   **C** never

2   Complete the profiles. Write *too much*, *enough* or *not enough*.

Your profile:

IF YOU CHOSE MOSTLY A

You have a very good lifestyle. You get [1] *enough* sleep and exercise, and you don't have [2]_____ junk food or coffee. You drink [3]_____ water and you eat [4]_____ fish.

IF YOU CHOSE MOSTLY B

Your lifestyle is OK. Try to do more exercise and stop eating fast food and sweets!

IF YOU CHOSE MOSTLY C

Your lifestyle is not very good for you. You have [5]_____ work and [6]_____ sleep. You don't drink [7]_____ water or eat [8]_____ fish. You eat [9]_____ junk food.

Over to you

Look at your
questionnaire
answers and write
your profile.
My lifestyle is quite
good. I eat ...

3 Complete the text about the changes in Anneke's life using the past simple of the verbs in the box.

eat get get get go have have ~~leave~~ move start take up

The choices I made

Anneke Kliegel, Switzerland, writes about the changes in her life and her hopes for the future.

I ¹ _left_ school when I was 16 and I ²_____ a job in a fast-food café. I ³_____ married to a lorry driver when I was 18 and ⁴_____ a baby when I was 19. I had a very unhealthy lifestyle – I ⁵_____ lots of junk food and didn't do any exercise, and I didn't use my brain. Then I ⁶_____ divorced from my husband and decided to change my life. I became a vegetarian and ⁷_____ yoga. I ⁸_____ to India for two years, where I ⁹_____ lessons in yoga and meditation. When I ¹⁰_____ back to Switzerland three years ago, I ¹¹_____ teaching yoga and stress management. I'm a much happier person now, and my daughter, Prisca, is happier, too.

In the future? I'm going to spend three months in India next summer, and I'm hoping to open my own yoga centre in a few years. And I'd like to have another child, a brother or sister for Prisca.

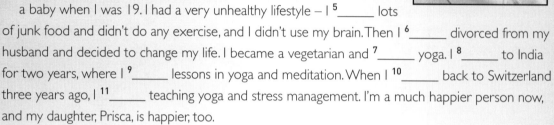

GRAMMAR
*be going to,
hoping to, would
like to*

4 Look at these people's hopes and plans for the future. Write *'m*, *'d* or *to* in the correct place.

I 'm hoping to go to university next year.

I'm going study in the States for six months.

I'm hoping get married in the future.

1 Thom

2 Gemma

3 Katrina

I like to take up a new sport, but I don't have time at the moment.

I going to start a new job next month.

I'd like have children in the future.

4 Kareem

5 Anne-Marie

6 Javier

Write three sentences about your hopes and plans. Use *I'm going to ...* , *I'm hoping to ...* and *I'd like to.*

5 Who is more certain of his/her plans?

1 Thom or Gemma?
2 Anne-Marie or Javier?

6 Luisa and Ruth are planning their holiday. Put the words in the correct order to complete the conversation.

LUISA OK, so ¹ are / what / we / about / to / do / going _what are we going to do about_ our holiday this year? We need to start planning.

RUTH I don't know. ² like / to / would / you / go / to / Where / ?
_____

LUISA Maybe somewhere like the north of Europe? Somewhere not too hot.

RUTH Good idea. When can you go? I can be free in June or July.
³ think / it's / too / I / busy _____
in August. And ⁴ really / accommodation / is / expensive.
_____

LUISA June ⁵ looks / me / to / good. _____ I'm not too busy then. What would you like to do when we're there?

RUTH ⁶sightseeing / to / like / I'd / do / some _____
and maybe relax, too.

LUISA Yeah, OK. Fine. Let's look at some websites this afternoon.

Time Out

7 Exercise your brain! Can you do these puzzles?

1 What's the missing letter?
J ? M A M J J A S O N D

2 Which is bigger: half of a quarter or a quarter of a half?

3 Cross out six letters. What word is left?
B S A I N X L E A T N T E A R S

4 What do an island and the letter T have in common?

5 What goes around the world but stays in a corner?

6 Put the letters in the right order. What do the words have in common?
T A R C O R   O O N I N   E T L E C T U   O T A O T P   C O B C R O I L

7 You have 50 spiders. How many legs and eyes do you have?

8 Write the two signs of the zodiac that contain these letters: COR

9 This sentense has two mistakes. What are they?

10 Some months have 30 days, some have 31. How many months have 28 days?

EXPLORE**Reading**

8   Read the web page on short holidays on page 79 and find the information.

1   Which holiday is the shortest?   ☐C☐
2   Which holiday is the longest?   ☐
3   Which holiday is the most expensive?   ☐
4   Which holidays can you NOT go on all year?   ☐ ☐ ☐
5   Which holidays include flights from the UK?   ☐ ☐
6   Which holidays can you ask for specially?   ☐ ☐

9   Are these sentences about the holidays true or false?

1   You can see mountains and the sea on holiday A.   ⓉRUE / FALSE
2   You only stay in bed and breakfasts on holiday B.   TRUE / FALSE
3   You don't stay in a hotel on holiday C.   TRUE / FALSE
4   You stay in a city on holiday D.   TRUE / FALSE
5   You stay in different places on holiday E.   TRUE / FALSE
6   You travel on a bus on holiday F.   TRUE / FALSE

10 Choose a holiday for each of these people.

1   Daniel is 28. He likes sports and nature and would like to visit the UK. He wants to go on holiday in May or June.
    Holiday ☐
2   Jess and Colin are a couple. He likes nature and animals. She enjoys going to the gym and relaxing. They live in the UK.
    Holiday ☐
3   Melanie and Serena are students. They want a sightseeing holiday that includes historical and natural sights. They would like to travel with a group.
    Holiday ☐
4   Ulrike is 43 and single. She can only have three or four days' holiday and wants to relax. She would like to meet the local people in the country she visits.
    Holiday ☐

11 Choose a holiday for Luisa and Ruth (see Exercise 6).

12 The web page asks people to review holidays they have been on. Look at what Kate Heneghan says and match the questions below (a–d) to her answers (1–4).

Read travellers' reviews

Reviewed 28 November by Kate Heneghan ★★★★★

1 It's difficult to say – the first sight of Petra, the crusader castle, sleeping under the stars … and how could I not mention the camel ride into the desert!

2 Book, go. Open your mind. Prepare to be amazed. Drink lots of bottled water. And take the minimum luggage needed.

3 The guides and drivers were all local, and the hotels were independently owned. We travelled as a group, so that cut down on petrol usage. We also travelled on specified routes through the Wadi Rum, so as not to disturb the nature, and they ensure there are rubbish facilities to keep the spaces clean.

4 Absolutely fantastic. It felt like a dream.

---

a   ☐ How would you rate your holiday overall?
b   ☐ What was the most memorable or exciting part of your holiday?
c   ☐ Did you feel that your holiday benefited local people and minimised impacts on the environment?
d   ☐ What tips would you give other travellers booking this holiday?

13 Which holiday did Kate go on?

14 Answer the questions in Exercise 12 about a holiday you've been on.

Over to you

Choose one of the holidays for you! Say where you would like to go and when.

www.short-breakholiday.com

Short-break holidays

Choose an original short-break holiday idea, weekend getaway, romantic short break or short-break adventure from specialist, responsible tour companies. All our short-break holidays are from the UK.

A Orca watching in Norway

in brief: North of the Arctic Circle are the Lofoten Islands. In November, when the days are short, and the Northern Lights often shine over the snow-covered mountains, this is one of the best places in the world to see these beautiful whales.

type of trip: Small group, November

price: From €990 (4 days) excl. flights

B Cycling holidays in England

in brief: A range of cycling breaks for people who want to explore England's countryside by bike. Accommodation in bed and breakfasts or small, family hotels.

type of trip: Small group, April–October

price: €265–€440 (3–5 days) excl. flights

C Provence cooking and walking holidays

in brief: Live with the local people and meet their friends in rural France, cook and eat regional products, see the beautiful countryside and experience French culture from the inside.

type of trip: All year on request

price: From €430 (2 days), excl. flights

D Birdwatching short break to Hungary

in brief: On the south slopes of the Bukk National Park in Eastern Hungary, Eger is the perfect place to see Hungary's spectacular bird life. Stay in a hotel with sauna, massage and fitness room.

type of trip: Small group, January–October

price: €285 (4 days), incl. UK flights

E Short break to St Petersburg, Helsinki and Tallinn

in brief: Enjoy three classic cities of the Finnish Gulf. Travel by local transport, stay in central hotels, see the most important sights, and meet local people.

type of trip: All year on request

price: From €750 (6 days), excl. flights

F Petra and Wadi Rum: short break to Jordan

in brief: From the capital, Amman, explore the hills and rocks of Wadi Rum valley by 4WD. Includes a visit to Kerak castle. Sleep in a Bedouin-style camp, then go to Petra, the ancient, rose-red city.

type of trip: Small group, all year

price: From €875 (5 days), incl. UK flights

THE LEARNING CENTRE
CITY & ISLINGTON COLLEGE
444 CAMDEN ROAD
LONDON N7 0SP
TEL: 020 7700 8642

1 Before you watch, match the activities (1–3) with the photos (a–c).

 **a**  **b**  **c**

1 parachuting ☐ 2 teaching English ☐ 3 making radio programmes ☐

2 Watch Mainda, Salvatore and Leo talking about what they are hoping to do in the future. Who talks about each activity? Write M (Mainda), S (Salvatore) or L (Leo).

1 parachuting ☐ 2 teaching English ☐ 3 making radio programmes ☐

Mainda

3 a Watch Mainda again (00:10–00:52). First tick (✓) the topics that she mentions.

health ☐ child care ☐ education ☐ work ☐

b Now tick (✓) the training she has done.

getting information for the programme ☐ using music ☐
structuring the programme ☐ presenting the programme ☐
working with sound ☐ asking good questions ☐

4 Watch Salvatore again (00:53–01:20) and (circle) the correct answers.

1 Salvatore has always wanted / decided recently to do a parachute jump.
2 He thinks it's frightening / exciting to see the world under you.
3 He is planning to do a solo jump / jump with an instructor.

Salvatore

5 Watch Leo again (01:21–02:06). Complete the text about his work and studies using the words in the box.

classroom learned opportunities teach training university ~~work~~

Leo started ¹___work___ as an English language teacher and later received full
²_____ and education from a ³_____ in the UK. He would like to use
what he has ⁴_____ at university in the ⁵_____ . He also thinks teaching
English as a foreign language gives teachers ⁶_____ to travel round the world.
He would love to ⁷_____ in Cambodia.

Leo

6 Can you remember what the people say? Match the beginnings and endings of the sentences. Watch the video again to help you.

Mainda
1 I am hoping to ...
Salvatore
2 I'm planning to ...
Leo
3 I would like to ...
4 I would really love to ...

a teach English.
b work at my community radio station.
c do it.
d apply what I've learned.

7 Describe something you hope to do in the future. Try to use some expressions from Exercise 6.

GLOSSARY

issues (plural noun): important subjects or problems that people are discussing
and so forth (expression): an expression that means *and things like that* or *etc.*
gather (**information**) (verb): to find and collect (information)
apply /əˈplaɪ/ (verb): to use something in a practical situation
in tandem (expression): If you do something **in tandem**, you do it at the same time as another person.

Acknowledgements

The authors would like to thank the editorial team in Cambridge, particularly Greg Sibley. Chris Cavey and Maggie Baigent would also like to thank Nick Robinson for his good humour, patience and ideas in his role as Project Manager in the earlier stages of the work. Many thanks also to Catriona Watson-Brown for her ever-thorough copy-editing.

Maggie Baigent would like to thank Michael Cotton for his loyalty and support.

Chris Cavey would like to thank Kate, Lily and Ella for their patience and support.

Nick Robinson would like to thank Anna Barnardo.

The authors and publishers are also grateful to the following contributors:

Design and page make-up: Stephanie White at Kamae Design
Picture research: Hilary Luckcock

The authors and publishers acknowledge the following sources of copyright material and are grateful for the permissions granted. While every effort has been made, it has not always been possible to identify the sources of all the material used, or to trace all copyright holders. If any omissions are brought to our notice, we will be happy to include the appropriate acknowledgements on reprinting.
Bell International for the extract on p12. Copyright © www.bell-centres.com/malta; Good Hope Studies for the extract on p12; Kirsty de Garis for the extract on p22, © Kirsty de Garis; Alice Fisher for the extract on p42. Copyright Guardian News & Media Ltd 2007; VSO, www.vso.org.uk, for the extract on p68.

The publisher has used its best endeavours to ensure that the URLs for external websites referred to in this book are correct and active at the time of going to press. However, the publisher has no responsibility for the websites and can make no guarantee that a site will remain live or that the content is or will remain appropriate.

The publishers are grateful to the following for the permissions to reproduce copyright photographs and material:

Key: l = left, c = centre, r = right, t = top, b = bottom

Alamy Images/©Jason Hosking for p4(b), /©Jason Hosking for p5(3), /Image Source Black for p5(bl), /©Radius Images for p5(br), /©Annette Price-H20 Photography for p6(cr), /©Ian Shaw for p6(br), /©Blend Images for p10, /©Cultura for p11(c), /©B L Images Ltd for p12(tl), /©S C Photos for p12(tc), /©Peter Treanor for p12(tr), /©Rubberball for p14(3), /©GoGo Images Corporation for p14(4), /©Profimedia International s.r.o. for p15, /©GlowImages for p16, /©North River Images for p19, /©David R Frazier Photolibrary Inc for p21, /©Westend61 for p26(r), /©Andrew Woodley for p29(t), /©GlowImages for p30, /©JupiterImages/Creatas for p34(tc), /©GlowImages for p34(bc), /©Blend Images for p34(br), /©Rohit Seth for p41, /©GoGoImages Corporation for p44(1), /©Uppercut Images for p44(2), /©Jim Powell for p44(3), /©Radius Images for p50(b), /©Robert Holmes for p53(t), /©Rubberball for p55(t), /©imagebroker for p55(ct), /©Buzzshotz for p55(cb), /©vario images GmbH & Co KG for p56(c), /©Adrian Lascom for p65(c), /©Phovoir/FCM Graphic for p65(bl), /©GoGo Images Corporation for p70(1), /©Rubberball for p70(3), /©Radius Images for p70(5), /Westend61 for p70(6) /©ImagesEurope for p73(tr); Corbis/©Wolf-zefa for p11(t), /©Darren Modricker for p27(l), /©Amanaimages for p46(tr), /©Image Source for p60(tl); Education Photos for pp34(bl), 44(4), 44(5), 44(b); Getty Images/©Iconica for p6(tl), /©GAB Archive/Redfern for p22(l), /©GAB Archive Redfern for p22(r), /© Harald Eisenberger for p24(b), /Harald Eisenberger for p26(l), /©Tom Bonaventure for p46(br), /©Daisuke Oka/Sebun Photo for p46(bl), /©Somos/Veer for p60(b), /©Larry Dale Gordon for p73(tc); Hannover Marketing & Tourismus GmbH for p24(c); istockphoto/©Jennifer London for p24(tr), /©G_studio for p34(tr), /©Byron W Moore for p45(t), /©James Cameron for p52, /©mseidlch for p55(b), /©Antonio D'Albore for p56(b), /©RainforestAustralia for p65(tr), /©sverx for p66(t), /©Contour99 for p70(2); Kobal Collection/©Lucas Film/Paramount Pictures for p49(r), /©RBT Stigwood Prods/Hemdale for p51(cl), /©MGM for p57(cr), /©Dreamworks for p51(b); Masterfile/©Norbert Schafer for p5(1), /©Artiga Photo for p5(2), /©John Gertz for p5(4), /©Tomas Rodriguez for p5(5), /©Tim Kuisalaas for p5(6), /©Norbert Schafer for p5(7), /©Kathleen Finlay for p5(8); Photolibrary/©PhotoDisc for p6(tr), /©PhotoDisc for p7, /©Cultura for p11(b), /©Uppercut Images for p14(2), /©Bananastock for p34(tl), /©Image Source for p36(r), /©Image Source for p37, /©PhotoDisc for p39(t), /©Uppercut Images for p44(6), /©Ambient Images for p45(b), /©imagebroker.net for p56(t), /©Image Source for p66(b), /©Radius Images for p70(4), /©Fancy for p70(t), /©Blend Images for p71, /©imagestate for p73(tl), /©F1 Online for p73(bl); Punchstock/©Valueline for p9, /©Digital Vision for p12(bl), /©Image Source for p14(1), /©Cultura for p14(5), /©PhotoDisc for p14(6); Rex Features/©Sony Pics/Everett for p51(t); Ronald Grant Archive/©Dreamworks for p49(l); Shutterstock/©Jonathon Brizendine for p13(br), /©Leah-Anne Thompson for p24(tl), /©Denis Babenko for p27(r), /©maribell for p32(l), /©Robyn Mackenzie for p32(r), /©Sklep Spozywczy for p33(l), /©Joe Gough for p33(r), /©Thomas Sztanek for p36(l), /©Andrew Gentry for p58(b), /©Yuri Arcurs for p59(b), /©Imagery/Majestic for p60(tr), /©Galvia Barskaya for p61, /©Orange Line Media for p63(tl), /©Kiselev Andrey Valerevich for p63(tcl), /©Phase4Photography for p63(tcr), /©Olga Kushcheva for p63(tr), /©Andrei Nekrassov for p73(bc), /©Regien Paassen for p73(br); Tom Craig for p42; Topfoto for p40(b).

Illustrations by Tom Croft, Mark Duffin, Clare Elsom, Kamae Design, Julian Mosedale, Nigel Sanderson, Sean Simms, Lucy Truman